Write Your Thesis in

6 Months

Using Strategic Thinking and the Kaizen Way

Book 1 of the Academic Publishing Success Series

Marcus B. Griffin, PhD &
Suzanne Griffin, PhD

Author Bios

Marcus B. Griffin, PhD completed his dissertation and doctoral studies in anthropology at the University of Illinois at Urbana-Champaign. He grew up in academia and helped his parents conduct ethnographic research in the Philippines in the 1970s and 1980s and later became an assistant and then associate professor of sociology and anthropology. He currently practices applied social science for corporate and government clients. As an entrepreneur, he is the co-founder of the AmericanProofreadingCenter.com and works with graduate students and university faculty to help them communicate their ideas effectively and publish their scholarship.

Suzanne Griffin, PhD completed her dissertation and doctoral studies in English Literature at Universiti Putra Malaysia. She was a university lecturer for fifteen years and currently is the managing director and co-founder of AmericanProofreadingCenter.com. Dr. Griffin is based in Tampa, Florida and regularly conducts workshops helping graduate students complete their dissertation and publish articles in reputable journals.

You can reach either Drs. Griffin & Griffin at editor@americanproofreadingcenter.com and can get tips and insight on how to write academic English well and get published by signing up for their newsletter at: https://americanproofreadingcenter.com

Dedication

We dedicate this book to the many students and faculty from around the world that we help through the American Proofreading Center. Your effort to communicate your scholarship to an English reading audience inspires us each day.

Table of Contents

Preface

When a teenager in the early 1980's, I* remember watching my father review and comment on dissertation chapters from his students at the University of Hawaii. There were often red marks on the pages. Sometimes he would mutter, "God, this is awful!" Other times at dinner, my father would complain about how long it was taking a student to write their thesis. My father always wanted me to become an anthropologist like him, and when I started writing my thesis in 1995, these memories of hearing his complaints about lack of progress or poor and irrelevant chapter sections haunted me.

When I started writing my thesis, I was literally scared of the task. In my fear of the unknown, I asked my supervisor how long he thought my thesis should be. He answered, "As long as it needs to be and not a word more!" Great. Only later did I appreciate what he meant. At the time I felt lost even though I grew up in academia and had participated in a lot of research. I consulted Kate L. Turabian's classic guide, *A Manual for Writers of Research Papers, Theses, and Dissertations*. It was such a long book! The amount of detailed instruction was almost confusing. I kept hearing my father's voice in my head, "God, this is awful!...Why is he taking so long to write?".

I was not the only graduate student haunted by the need to write a dissertation. You may be haunted by it too. You are definitely not alone.

When my co-author, Dr. Suzanne Griffin, was working on her dissertation at the Universiti Putra Malaysia, there were so many students suffering with this problem. One classmate was struggling so much he started seeing a psychotherapist. I was really glad to hear he did that because sometimes a student who does not get professional help does something terrible to himself.

This struggle can last for years. My father had students who took ten years to complete their dissertation and finally earn their PhD. When Dr. Suzanne started her PhD journey, she met a woman who finished her coursework after two years but after five more years was still trying to complete her thesis. Her supervisor kept sending her chapters back for more and more revisions.

I struggled to write my thesis for the first two months and rewrote my introductory chapter five times. My situation did not change until I remembered John R. Trimble's book, *Writing with Style: Conversations on the Art of Writing*. I previously used it during an advanced expository writing class as a senior undergraduate. In his book, now in its third edition, he provides lots of great advice on how to write well. But one technique in particular really captured my attention.

Dr. Trimble talked about using half sheets of paper to write one idea at a time as a way to improve the writing process. For him, a writer should create a handful of half-sheets of paper, each with one idea on it elaborated into a paragraph. Doing this breaks down the problem of writer's block. Then, a writer should sit down with the sheets of paper, read them, shuffle them, then read them again. After three or four readings, you set the half-sheets of paper aside and free-write a full draft of the ideas without looking at the half-sheets of paper. The result is a synthesis of the pages and the words are in your own words, no quotes and no plagiarism.

I adapted this technique to my own purpose and it changed my experience writing my dissertation. This book is built on Dr. Trimble's technique along with several other techniques for writing relevant content for your thesis.

Without these techniques, writing a Master's or PhD thesis will not be easy. In fact, it likely will be very hard. Writing a thesis can give you high blood pressure, gray hair and regular headaches. Some graduate students end up divorced before they finish their thesis. But it does not have to be this way!

With the strategy and techniques we provide you in this book,

- You will enjoy your thesis writing journey and your quest to obtain a Master's degree or PhD.

- Writing your thesis will be a journey of discovery and a time in which you will thrive.
- With this book as your guide, you will not get gray hair (at least from writing your thesis).

Let's get started!

*A note on author's voice in our book: Though we co-wrote this book, we decided that the author's voice will primarily be one perspective and the use of "I" refers to Marcus. Collective ideas are referred to as "we" and we mark Suzanne's perspective by saying "Suzanne" or "Dr. Suzanne". This approach sounds better and is more concise.

PART ONE

Abundance through strategy

We live in a world characterized by accelerating change. No matter how much we get done, there always seems more than must be done. So much remains that we often cannot feel satisfaction for the things we completed. Despite smartphone time management apps, cloud-based time trackers and integrated project completion charts, we barely survive. But no matter your pace of work, you can finish your thesis in six months by approaching it using strategy and an integrated set of methods that build continuous improvement.

In this chapter, we will explain the strategy and methods that enable you to write a good quality thesis in six months. Our strategy and set of methods are not hype. They are real. I used this strategy and some of the methods in 1995 to write my thesis in six months. When I sat for my oral defense (the American version of the British system's viva voce), I walked away with a pass and minor corrections. The corrections were few. I completed them in one month. Suzanne used this same strategy and completed her thesis draft in good time as well. When we sat down to write this book, we completed the first draft in ONE MONTH using this strategy.

We did not invent the individual methods given to you in the following

1

pages. But we did synthesize them into an original strategy. The strategy is based on a coordinated way of using each method to maximize your ability to write good content for your thesis. You will also use this strategy to write future research proposals, journal articles and books. For example, you will use a concept mapping program called Scapple coupled with a writing program called Scrivener, both from Literature and Latte.

You need to memorize and use the techniques in the strategy until they become a natural framework for writing. Your mastery should become much like the individual tasks and skills required of driving a car. You probably no longer think about foot pressure on the brake pedal as you push the turn signal, turn the steering wheel, and look for cross traffic and the lane to stay within while you enter an intersection with a green light giving you the right of way. In time you will not think all the time about your writing strategy. You will just do it just like you "just drive". The results will be obvious in the form of pages written each day that mark progress on your journey to completing your PhD.

The techniques that make up the strategy are:

Kaizen: using small steps to continuously improve and create big results

Pomodoro (aka Pom): 25 minutes of focused activity followed by five minutes of rest before starting another "Pom"

Pareto's Principle (aka 80/20 rule): 20 percent of action or effort accounts for 80 percent of outcome or productivity

Important-Urgent Matrix: a quadrant that helps you to distinguish what truly needs to be done and when compared against what is not important and therefore probably not worth doing no matter how urgent it may seem

Software: computer and mobile devise applications that improve your writing, time management, and effectiveness

Your Writing Space: the places you use or the spaces you create to write productively

Writing Project Box: a plastic crate that contains and tames your writing materials so it does not feel like your thesis is taking over your life

Let's learn more about each of these techniques to maximize your writing productivity and quality.

The 80/20 Rule or The Pareto Principle

An important element in your strategy to write your thesis in six months is maximizing your gains by taking advantage of the 80/20 Rule, otherwise called the Pareto Principle. It was developed by Vilfredo Pareto in the mid-1800s. The principle is that 80% of results comes from 20% of action. The principle is a ratio that can be seen in many facets of life and nature. Stories about Pareto say that he noticed that 80% of pea production in his garden came from only 20% of his pea plants. Having grown peas myself because I love gardening, I find that hard to believe, but maybe pea seeds were of poor quality back then. Then Pareto noticed that 80% of land in Italy was owned by 20% of the population and 20% of companies were responsible for 80% of production. That I can believe because 80% of the world's wealth is owned by 20% of its population. This pattern is therefore commonly called the 80/20 rule. There are a number of other ways this rule seems to show up today:

20% of employees produce 80% of results in an office

20% of customers account for 80% of sales

20% of manufacturing defects cause 80% of customer complaints

20% of patients consume 80% of healthcare spending

It is spooky where you can find this pattern. I live in a ten room house but really only live in three of them (almost 20%--it is not a hard ratio). Suzanne has a lot of clothes but only wears approximately 20% of them (there are a few sets that she just keep choosing; she does not know why). I have five fishing rods but only really use one of them even if I take three with me to the river or ocean to fish (I just really like how that one rod and reel feels in my hands and its ability to sense a fish biting). We have many, many clients that use our journal writing and thesis editing consulting services through AmericanProofreadingCenter.com, but really only 20% of our customers provide us with consistent income (maybe we do not try hard enough with the occasional clients). Suzanne has 36 apps on her smartphone, but only uses eight regularly (22%!—why not delete the others??). We could think of more examples from our lives, but you get the point. Let's apply the rule to your life now.

You can apply the 80/20 rule to many aspects of your life. In principle, 80% of your productivity will come from 20% of your effort. So what are those things you are doing to produce most of your results and what are the other things you are doing 80% of the time that are unproductive? You probably can get rid of most of them and not have a noticeable decline in your productivity but massive increase in your available time and energy. 20% of your spending likely brings 80% of your joy and satisfaction. 20% of classes you took in college and graduate school probably account for 80% of what you learned and found meaningful. 20% of your friends and family members provide you with 80% of your support and assistance while on your quest to get a Master's degree or PhD. That means 80% of your classes were mostly a waste of time, 80% of your spending needs to be rethought (more savings!), and 80% of friends and family really do not do much to help you get through this endurance test called a PhD--they are just sort of "there". There are ways to improve on this (see the section on friends and family and the section on your supervisor for more information). But for now, let's apply this to your writing.

Without using our strategy, only 20% of your writing will be used in your PhD or Master's thesis. Let's say 25% of your writing will account for 100% of your final thesis. This may sound depressing, but it isn't really. Once you know to be on the lookout for "wasted" writing, you can become more efficient and relevant in your writing. There are whole sections that you might write that will never be used. What anguish! But imagine giving your supervisor irrelevant material to read and comment on. Now you have an irritated supervisor that gives you depressing comments that slow your writing and delay your completion, not to mention giving you high blood pressure, a desire to overeat, and grey hair.

The Pareto principle is not an immutable fact of life. You are not condemned to 80% wasted, unproductive effort. Identify the unproductive 80% and expand on the productive 20% and you will get more done in less time with greater effect. Our strategy helps you to dramatically increase how much of your writing ends up in your final thesis. This amount will probably be around 80% of all your writing.

With this in mind, we will teach you how to approach writing your PhD thesis using a system of coordinated elements: our strategy. These elements together maximize your output and reduce wasted or unproductive effort. For example, using Scapple to concept map (not outline!) your writing, you will identify the concepts and chapter elements that are most relevant and important to write. You will not waste time, energy, emotion, and effort writing content that is not likely going to be used. More and more of what you write will end up in your first draft and your final thesis. With more of what you write finding its place in your thesis, you will write less overall. No more 80% waste. No more irritated supervisor having to read irrelevant material. No more overeating and grey hair because you have more time to exercise to beat the stress you do have, eat nice meals with friends and family, and enjoy your PhD journey.

Let's start applying the Pareto principle to your daily and weekly routine. You want to create a high-impact routine. Thinking about how you go about your day requires honesty. Follow the instruction of Polonius in Shakespeare's Hamlet: "To thine own self be true." Let's jump in with being honest about when we are smartest.

Which times of the day are you most mentally alert? Can you match those times of the day with when you can write material for your thesis? If the time you have available to write is not exactly when you are most mentally alert, can you make changes in your behavior to promote alertness? The goal is to write your thesis when your brain is at its best. A sleepy brain will not produce very good writing. A tired body is not helpful when sitting in a chair with a laptop or desktop computer while trying to write. Producing academic prose that will more likely than not find a place in your thesis requires you to figure this out.

Even if your most alert time for writing is not available, you can train yourself to make the necessary 2-3 hours that are available to you productive. But if peak mental alertness time is available to you, seize it for writing. The result will be relevant and quality writing that will find a place in your thesis and lead to satisfying results from your supervisor and examiners. Let's see more about the crucial role of routine and rewards in the next section on habits to help make the most of the 80/20 rule.

The Power of Habits

Even if you have a strategy and you have the techniques we provide you, they will be ineffective if you do not understand the role of habits in your life and how to reshape your habits rather than be a victim of your habits. Habits are those things we do routinely and without much thinking about them. What you want is a set of habits that lead you to writing your thesis in six months. There is much more to this goal than sitting down and writing. That approach is working harder, not smarter. By making your habits clear to yourself and seeing how you want to be (visualize your printed thesis in your hands and a goofy smile of relief and joy on your face), you can make new habits and overcome old habits that do not align with your goals. Sound too good to be true? Not really. You came to the habits you perform daily now, why not have other habits instead? With the kaizen approach described in the next section and a bit of self-reflection, you will get the habits you need to write your thesis (and more!) in six months. Let's look more closely at habits to see how this will work.

The first step in creating new habits is to realize that we make habits. In Charles Duhigg's book, The Power of Habit, he states that:

"Once you know a habit exists, you have the responsibility to change it...and once you understand that habits can change, you have the freedom and the responsibility to remake them. Once you understand that habits can be rebuilt, the power of habit becomes easier to grasp and the only option left is to get to work."

We know habits exist. For example, my habit is to get up in the morning, use the toilet, wash my hands, wash my face, go to the kitchen, start a pot of coffee, drink a glass of water, and then contemplate how much I hate mornings. Everyday. That sequence of actions is a habit and I do not stop to think after washing my face, "I wonder what I should do next?" Once I have at least one cup of coffee, then my brain starts wondering about what is next.

I recently took a job that required me to be at work by 530am. Knowing I had a habit, my routine slightly changed from a working-from-my home-office routine to a routine that had me at work by 530. This new routine had me getting up at 4am, getting dressed into work clothes after the first cup of coffee (still not really much thinking happening yet), pouring a second cup of coffee in my car-safe cup and driving away to work (brain is now functioning and I am either listening to an audiobook or jamming out with Daft Punk playing loudly in the car). I made my morning habit. I can change it.

You can change your habits also for the better, but often procrastination gets in the way of change. You know you need to write every day to be a successful academic and to complete your thesis. You plan to write today, but something comes up. Something urgent comes along. Or you just don't feel like it and postpone doing it until "later". Later keeps being later and then it is night time and you find yourself getting ready for bed without having written a word. Day after day after day. Weeks go by and you still have not written much of anything. This discourages you and you keep telling yourself, "I really should be writing!" But your other habits keep channeling you into other tasks and priorities.

There are many books about solving the procrastination problem, but we encourage you to focus on two activities as it relates to writing your thesis. The first is to embrace kaizen. The second is to embrace using Pomodoros. Both are fully described later in this chapter. Think small gains by writing kaizen notes. Then think time on task, not completion of anything, so that you convert kaizen notes into paragraphs and pages 25 minutes at a time. You can write a kaizen note about some ideas in your thesis while you are standing in the checkout line waiting to pay for your groceries or sitting in the train or bus going home from the university. You can find 25 minutes to work on elaborating on your kaizen notes. Start small and use Poms. Procrastination gets crushed with the one-two punch of kaizen and Pomodoros. Develop these two practices together into a new habit. Other productive habits will follow. This is called strategy.

But let's dig a little deeper about the power of habits and how they form behavioral loops. We will build off of Duhigg's book, The Power of Habit because it is THE book on habit formation and change. You can explore others later. You can read Duhigg's book if you want later. For now we will keep it simple so you can write your thesis in six months.

Habits are Cue, Routine and Reward Loops

Habits occur based on a series of three things: cue, routine and reward. My morning routine starts by waking up naturally or by hearing my 4am alarm go off. Man, I hate that alarm! With that cue, my routine set of behaviors follows. I described them earlier. My reward kicks in and can be seen in several increments. I feel relieved after using the toilet. I feel clean after washing my hands and face, my eyes feel less dry and scratchy after drinking a glass of water, and I start to wake up and feel alert once I start drinking my first cup of coffee. Cue, routine, reward. Cue, routine, reward. Cue, routine, reward. The more frequently you do it, the more stuck in the series of things we become. It is a loop we follow without thinking too much.

To change your habits, you only need to change the routine that follows the cue. You do not have to change everything. Change the routine, and you will change your habit. If you are trying to create a habit, think in terms of cue, routine, reward to make the habit stick.

To do this, create a cue. Maybe it is coming back from dropping off your child to school. Maybe it is arriving in your office. Maybe it is washing the last dish in the sink after dinner. Let's use that one as an example. After washing the last dish (your cue), you need to start your routine of writing. Sit down for 25 minutes and write (doing a Pom). After 25 minutes, your timer pulls you out of The Zone and you take a short break for some kind of reward. Whatever that reward is, when you strategically design your cue, routine, and reward as a loop, you will build a habit of writing that will stick with you. The more you do it, the more it becomes what your brain and body expect.

Keep in mind the power of habits, design your habits by being smart about setting up cues, routines and rewards. Do this and you will have less and less mental resistance to writing your thesis every day. Also, keep in mind that you are not trying to write your thesis in one day but rather through the use of kaizen notes during Pom sessions. Let's take a closer look now at kaizen notes and then Poms.

Kaizen

As we said at the start of this chapter, you will write your PhD or Master's thesis in six months using a strategy comprised of several coordinated techniques. One of those techniques is kaizen. It is a Japanese word that literally means "good change" and generally means continuous improvement using small steps to achieve big results. Kaizen can and is used for many improvements. Instead of trying to dramatically change your habits and life (which rarely works in the long run), kaizen shows you how to make small, even ridiculously small, changes in what you do. These changes lead to transformation and are enduring.

To write your dissertation, you are going to start by using what we call kaizen notes. These are small pieces of paper that have only one or two sentences on them. Sometimes they just have a phrase. No piece of paper has more than one main idea on it. If you have more than one idea on your mind, write a second kaizen note. And a third. And a fourth. You will discover that throughout the day, you will end up writing more than a dozen kaizen notes. These notes with one sentence on them, maybe two sentences, turn into paragraphs when you sit down to write each day. These paragraphs then turn into pages each day. Using kaizen notes to jump start your writing sessions, each week you will have more than a dozen pages of thesis text. In six months, you will have at least 300 pages written, if not much more. Kaizen: small continuous steps lead to big results. That is how it works to help you write your thesis in six months. The use of kaizen is explained in detail when we describe your daily writing time in the section called Building Chapters. To make kaizen notes work well in your daily writing, you need to incorporate them into Pomodoros.

The Pomodoro Technique of Focused Effort

How you write is as important as what you write if you want to be consistently productive. One technique you should use to write your thesis in six months is called the Pomodoro. It involves 25 minutes of focused effort followed by a five minute break and then another 25 minutes of writing. If you want to make your "Poms" 50 minutes with a ten minute break, go for it. We do not recommend going longer than 50 minutes though. Giving your brain a short break lets it work better than if you work for long periods with no break. The point of using Poms is that by using them, you have a block of time that you focus exclusively on one task: in this case writing.

Using the Pomodoro technique is simple. Get a timer and set it to 25 minutes. I use a Star Wars Death Star timer that makes a laser cannon sound when the time is up. You can use a timer app on your smart phone like Suzanne, your watch if it has a timer, or use an app on your computer. Whatever you like is what you should use. Set your timer and focus only on your writing. You will be using your kaizen notes to start typing and turn sentences into paragraphs and paragraphs into pages, so do not worry at this point about writer's block and looking at a blank computer screen for 25 minutes.

You have your kaizen notes in front of you and you know where the content you write will fit into your thesis because you concept-mapped your outline in detail using Scapple (this is explained in the chapter on software you need). You also are keeping it all organized in the writing application, Scrivener. Remember, you are using Poms as part of your systematic method for producing a thesis in six months. Elements in your system are not independent of each other. They work together to produce fast, relevant results. You have your notes and you know where the ideas fit in your thesis and this knowledge prevents writer's block and helps to make the ideas flow out of your mind and onto the page.

When your timer goes off, take a five minute break. You should stretch your body. If you want, center your *chi* (energy—Google it) afterward with a two minute *dan tien* meditation after stretching. You might reward yourself with a cup of green tea to reinforce the habit loop of que, routine, reward (as discussed earlier in this chapter). When that is finished, set your timer again and resume writing for another 25 minutes.

You will pick up where you left off. I frequently leave the sentence I was writing incomplete when the timer goes off. You should too. Read the paragraph you were writing to refresh your mind where you were conceptually in the text and finish the sentence previously left incomplete. In addition to using your kaizen notes, you will be using the SEE-I writing format to help you create well-structured paragraphs and pages (SEE-I is explained in the chapter on building chapters). Using kaizen notes and the SEE-I format within two 25 minute Poms or one 50 minute Pom, you will create at least one page of text. Trust me. You probably will create two pages, but we will remain conservative in our estimate for now. After one and a half or two hours of focused writing, you will complete your daily two-page minimum.

Two pages a day, every day, results in 14 pages of thesis text per week. In two weeks, you will have 28 pages of thesis text. 25-30 pages is the preferred length for a thesis chapter. You produced a thesis chapter's worth of text in two weeks! Hang on though. In one month, you will have written a minimum of 56 pages when writing two pages a day based on four, 25 minute Poms. Remember, we are being conservative. You may have written 75 pages in four weeks. In six months, you will have written a minimum of 336 pages of thesis text, which is longer than most theses need to be. Yay! Time to celebrate how small, daily gains lead to huge results and transformational outcomes. Kaizen!

Before we get too excited, let's come back to what we said regarding the Pareto principle. The rule is that 20% of your effort will result in 80% of your productivity; seen in reverse this means that 80% of your effort will contribute to only 20% of your productivity. By using the systematic and coordinated method we are providing you, working smart lets you eliminate most of the wasted effort. Your first thesis draft will have at least 336 pages of text THAT YOU WROTE and UNDERSTAND. You might have 500 pages after six months. With that draft, you can now edit it down, making it more concise. We will talk more later about the role of editing in producing a great thesis draft. For now we are pointing out that your two page minimum per day on two hours of focused writing results in everything you need to complete your thesis in six months. Period.

Distractions Kill Complete Focus

Distraction-free writing is hard to enforce, however. Doing a Pomodoro is not as easy as sitting down for 25 minutes and writing. As you will hear us say many times, simple is not the same as easy. But why is sitting for 25 minutes so hard? If we look closely at our habits and our environment, we will find the source of many distractions and take steps to limit their impact on our effort to write 25 minutes at a time.

First off, we often think we are more focused than we really are. While reading this page, do you have your cell phone on? Are you near a computer with email open or an internet browser showing your

Facebook feed? Have you been checking your phone messages or multitasking by having a chat on WhatsApp while you read this? Are you at work and reading this but answering the phone or making a PowerPoint presentation at the same time? Complete focus is, in fact, quite rare today. But it is crucial to writing your thesis in six months.

Complete focus is needed because writing good thesis content requires you to get into what we call "The Zone". It is a mental state where you are living in the ideas in your head and not thinking much about anything other than the ideas in your head. The Zone is a really cool place to be and very productive. Coming out of The Zone is mentally uncomfortable. For this reason, some thesis coaches encourage graduate students to write for 50 minutes at a time. If coming out of The Zone is too uncomfortable and you do not like the in and out caused by the five minute break between Poms, go for 50 minutes. Complete focus though created by a 25 minute or 50 minute Pom enables you to immerse yourself in your thesis subject. The words flow like a video unfolding in front of you when you are in The Zone. You are more productive and your work is at its best quality. Preventing distractions can be hard but are necessary to achieving what is truly important: writing your thesis.

Focused writing time is important to getting your thesis written in six months. You need to identify what normally distracts you when you are trying to work. Make a list of all the distractions you encounter today while going about your normal day. You can even try doing Poms today and see what interrupts you. Write them down today. Tonight, go through your list and see what most frequently interrupts you. Each kind of interruption is a problem. Together the kinds of interruptions are a system of problems. Some of them will be the biggest problems, others less so. Now make a list of solutions that might prevent each kind of interruption. Identify which are the most effective solutions solving the biggest problems. You now have a prioritized system of solutions that minimize the impact of your system of problems. You just applied the Pareto principle to your problem with interruptions by identifying the 20% of solutions that will cancel 80% of your interruption problems. With your systemic approach to problem setting and solution framing, now you can put the solutions in place prior to doing your thesis writing. Once in place, the system of solutions catches most of the things that will interrupt your Pom and drag you out of The Zone.

Pomodoros Kill Procrastination

There is another benefit and use of Poms when writing your thesis (or doing any other task you want to avoid, like grading student papers, or drafting a proposal outline, or commenting on a writing buddy's manuscript). Poms give you a way to overcome procrastination because you focus on time, not the completion of a task. You may not want to work on drafting a proposal outline because you think of it in terms of completion or outcome. With a Pom, you can tell yourself that you do not need to finish the task, you just need to work on it for 25 minutes. We can deal with all kinds of unpleasant tasks for just 25 minutes. If you must, give yourself an incentive for doing it like a cookie or a walk around the neighborhood or even watching a video of grumpy cat to make you laugh. Or you can reward yourself with reading a section of novel (that is what I usually do). Design your habit, once again, by taking seriously your brain's desire for rewards. You set your distraction prevention measures in place (cue) and dive in for 25 minutes on a task (routine) you would otherwise have made excuses to avoid. 25 minutes later you are laughing at something on social media and satisfied (reward) because you got more done in half an hour at high quality than often you get done in two hours of distracted effort that may end in the trash or editing bin.

Sometimes we procrastinate because we do not want to deal with a thesis section that is hard or somehow unpleasant. Mark Twain once said, "Eat a live frog first thing in the morning and nothing worse will happen to you the rest of the day." What he meant by this is you need to tackle the most important task of your day first. Often we do not want to tackle it and work on less important tasks, procrastinating until the important task becomes an urgent priority that stresses you out. Procrastination is like a distraction and you can overcome it using Poms. Remind yourself that you only need to work on the difficult or unpleasant thesis section or topic for 25 minutes. Set up your distraction prevention measures and set your timer for 25 minutes (cue), swallow that frog (routine), and when the timer bell chimes, reward yourself (reward).

Knowing about Poms, kaizen, the power of habits, or the 80/20 rule is not enough. You also need to maximize time and energy doing things that are important no matter how urgent other things may be. Let's explore the urgent:important matrix to better understand where you are spending your time and energy. Your goal is to live in the important but not urgent zone of writing your thesis. Let's see how to make this happen in the next section.

The Urgent:Important Matrix

Another way to use the Pareto principle is to think carefully not just about when you are most mentally alert, but if you are doing the right, important things most of the time. Steven Covey's four quadrants of effectiveness is a crucial framework to use if you want to be effective with less effort and stress. Covey described and outlined his four quadrants in his book, The 7 Habits of Highly Effective People, originally published in 1989 and later in his book, First Things First.

Being effective and making the most of your time and effort involves identifying how you go about your day, day after day. Days build weeks and weeks build months, which in turn build years. So we are focused right now on how you spend your day. While being honest with yourself, ask yourself:

- Are you primarily doing the right things during each day? How do you know they are the right things?
- Are they your right things or someone else's urgent need or priority?
- Are you avoiding effectiveness by wasting your time with excessive entertainment and trivial tasks that are neither important nor urgent?
- Do you have a feeling that you are busy all day long getting urgent things done yet feeling empty that you can't get enough done?
- Do you wish you could work on a project idea that you know would make a real difference but cannot seem to find the time to fit it into your hectic and stressed out schedule?
- Are you seeing days go by and wondering when you will get your next thesis chapter finished?

You are not alone. We bet most people around you at home, school, and work are also feeling this way. Covey provides a framework solution.

There are things that are either important or they are not important. Some things are more important than others and you can argue that tasks, goals, projects, and things to do fall on a continuum from very important to not at all important. Great. We will get to how important or unimportant later when we discuss the principles that guide your choices. But for now, keep importance binary. Things you do are either important or they are not important. End of story. Make a choice. Only you can decide. Is what you are doing important or not?

Now ask yourself is what you are doing urgent or not urgent? Do you have to do it right now? Do you want or feel it needs to be done right now?

Why not later? If you did not do it right now, what would happen? Is the task urgent for you or urgent for someone else? Is someone else's poor planning now an emergency for you? How did it become urgent?

Remember, "To thine own self be true." Answer honestly. This is hard stuff. You may not like facing reality. You may prefer to think you are being time efficient and effective when in fact you are not. People often do not face the truth because that would likely require them to change their behavior and way of thinking. Change is uncomfortable. So people delude themselves and carry on with the same habits and choices day after day. Someone important long ago said, "The truth will set you free." Let's put that statement to the test and organize what you do each day and week into the four quadrants created by our two dimensions of important and urgent.

Quadrant 1: Important and Urgent

Quadrant 2: Important and Not Urgent

Quadrant 3: Urgent but Not Important

Quadrant 4: Not Urgent and Not Important

Simple. We like simple. Unfortunately, simple is not always easy. Being honest about where our time, talent and treasure are placed in each of the quadrants is not easy despite being simple. It is uncomfortable and you might be tempted to avoid doing it. Don't. Let's do it.

Important and Urgent tasks are common in our lives. We spend a lot of time doing these kinds of tasks. We spend a lot of money responding to them and experience a lot of stress. This is not a fun quadrant to dwell in. Some people thrive in this quadrant though and may be addicted to the stress hormones that occur when doing important and urgent tasks. They may love the social drama at home or in the office that can occur. They may crave the high-speed car race that characterizes urgent and important tasks. They may be addicted to the attention that follows from "saving the day". The sad fact is, however, that most things that fall into the important and urgent quadrant get there because of someone's poor planning, procrastination, work avoidance, and lack of leadership. We are not talking about medical emergencies that arise from car accidents or landslides. Medical staff treating a gunshot wound in the emergency room are on an important and urgent mission to save someone's life. We are talking about a report that was not adequately developed and staffed, and now it must be completed by close of business TODAY. We are talking about avoiding an article re-submission deadline because you did not feel like re-writing the hard sections and now the deadline is tomorrow. As a result you are living in the important and urgent quadrant by staying up all night trying to finish the article. Because you have so many meetings on your daily calendar, emails that must be answered, paperwork to complete, and appointments to keep you are too exhausted from being busy to exercise even though you know exercise is important. It is just not urgent like so many pressing demands in your hectic life. The important and urgent quadrant crushes you and prevents you from completing your thesis in a timely manner and prevents you from enjoying your PhD journey and your life.

The urgent but not important quadrant is also an unpleasant space to be in. The tasks you do in this quadrant are those things that are urgent and you do them because they are urgent. You feel the need to do them because many times you may feel important by all the urgent things you get done. The urgency creates an illusion that the tasks or activities are important. If it wasn't urgent, how could it possibly not be important too? So you dive in and work on getting them done in time. If you step back from the urgent nature of most of the tasks in this quadrant, you will start to see that you are deceived about importance. In fact, most of the tasks are important to someone else, not you. Someone stops by to talk with you and you stop what you are doing because they are right in front of you wanting your time NOW. Or they call you and expect you to answer your phone regardless of what you are doing, even if what you are doing is truly important. Most meetings are urgent in the sense that they have a start time, but they are not important. They are office rituals that give the illusion of collaboration when information sharing is all that usually happens. A summary email or status report filled in by each staff section likely would easily replace most meetings and take one tenth the amount of time and can be safely ignored by 80% of staff that get the emailed report. People use much of their precious time, even their best brain-alertness time, attending to other people's priorities and urgencies and do so thinking they are in the important and urgent quadrant. Getting over your need to please and be available will go a long way to eliminating wasted time on work that is urgent but not important to your goals and priorities. Yay! More time and energy will be available for you to work on your thesis!

Quadrant 4 is another area where you can get back time and energy for writing your thesis and other important tasks like cooking a meal with your loved ones. Quadrant 4 is the zone of not important and not urgent. You might ask yourself, "Why would I be in this quadrant if I know the activities are not important and not demanding my attention right now?" Good question. The answer is work avoidance, procrastination, and a desire to be entertained leads you to consume huge amounts of time in Quadrant 4. Remember Facebook? I'm not hating on it, but think about how frequently you browse your feed or explore different groups NOT to stay in touch with people important to you, but to KILL time and otherwise distract yourself. Was the three minute video of grumpy cat that your friend shared really important? No. Was it urgent? No. What was going to be a quick peek at Facebook ended up taking 20 minutes before you refocused on other things. The same thing can be said of YouTube and SnapChat viewing. We have an addiction to be entertained and distracted to relieve our stress from being stuck in Quadrant 1 doing important and urgent tasks and Quadrant 3 doing urgent but not important (to us) tasks. You can recover huge amounts of time if you step back and critically examine your need for entertainment, distraction, and the desire to please other people. Remember how you thought you did not have time to write your thesis? Guess what? Now you have more time than you need to write it. And you will do it by spending as much time as possible in Quadrant 2, the important but not urgent zone.

Good planning, focusing on what is of value to you, and maintaining your boundaries against intrusions that are not important leads to significant productivity and effectiveness. This zone is also not full of stress. The only zone with less stress is perhaps the zone of unimportant and not urgent, but only because you are usually entertaining yourself with videos, pointless emails, text chats, or spacing out on social media.

Fight to dwell primarily in the important but not urgent Quadrant 2 so you can work on what matters most in your life with the greatest amount of energy and pleasure possible. All it takes is some honesty, critical thinking, and creative problem-solving to get others to respect what is important to you. Of course, we do not live in isolation from others and what is important to them. In fact, to write a good thesis in six months, you need a network of healthy relationships with family, friends, classmates, faculty, and administrative staff (never, ever underestimate how much you need the help and kindness of your graduate secretary and other support staff!!). Good relationships are maintained, not simply created, and you can nurture them by respecting other people's important but not urgent priorities and asking them to do the same for you.

All these ideas are great, but you need technology tools also. Let's switch from mental tools to software tools you need to get the most out of your effort and time.

PART TWO

Software You Need

The mental tools of the strategy given to you to complete your thesis in six months are not enough. You need technology tools as well. These technology tools are:

Trello: to help you organize and keep track of your individual tasks

Evernote: to help you easily capture and manage information from the internet and information on whiteboards, books in a library, and elsewhere

Endnote: to quickly build and maintain a library of references and digital copies of articles you use in your thesis literature review, chapters, and journal articles you write based on your thesis project

Scapple: to help you concept map your ideas and find relationships among ideas in your thesis project

Scrivener: to help you write your thesis by providing not only a word processing canvas, but also by making it easy to move thesis sections and keep track of your whole writing project in one, affordable software program.

Let's look at each technology tool in detail so you know why you need each and how you will use them together to write your thesis.

Trello

Trello is an online application that lets you manage your thesis or journal writing and publication tasks using a workflow approach instead of a checklist approach. You start with a board, which you can think of as a cork board that you might pin cards onto. Each card you create has the name of a task you need to complete. You can have as many cards as you want.

Your cards should be ordered in columns to create sets of cards that can be moved from one column to the next. You do not want a mess of cards on your board. To maximize your workflow, which is how you manage one task to the next, and make your task management logical and useful, create a set of cards (each containing a task) called "Urgent Top Priority". This is the stack of cards that you must get done right away and capture the things that fall in your Urgent and Important quadrant. This is the first column of cards on your board and goes to the far left of your board/screen. The next column of cards you create is the set you use to create new tasks, things you need to get done. This column is called, "To Do Work". This set can become a long column of cards, so take it easy at first. The third column should be called "Doing". This is the set of cards you are actively working on today. You will drag cards from your To Do Work column and drop them in the Doing column. The column to the right of this is your fourth column and is called "Done". This is your happiest column. It contains a running list of all the tasks (represented as cards) you completed today, yesterday, this week, and this past month. To fill it, you will drag and drop a card from the Doing column to the Done Column. At some point you will archive cards in this column, but not in the first month. Your next column is called "Emails to do". You want a separate column for email tasks because email is such a drain on your thesis and journal writing efforts. Keep emails you need to write separate from your list of other things to do found in other columns. Your next-to-last column is your "Delegated Tasks" column. It contains all those tasks that can be safely delegated to someone else, such as a coworker, personal/research assistant, or another student. Your final column on the far right of your screen is called, "Trashed for Another Life". These are the cards that once sat in the To Do Work column but never made it to Doing and never became important enough to find a home in the Urgent Top Priority column. You do not want to simply delete the card and give up on the task. Put it in the column of cards that you would get to if you had another life.

The genius of this arrangement in Trello is that cards can be dragged

18

and dropped from one column to another. For example, you made a card called "Rewrite abstract". It sat in the To Do Work column until you couldn't ignore it. In a fit of optimism after a cup of tea, you dragged it from the To Do Work column and dropped it into the Doing column. You wrote three or four sentences. Then you were distracted by the phone. Or you went on Facebook to avoid the discomfort of writing the abstract. The following day you dragged it back to To Do Work. Two weeks later, you've got to submit the article that needs the abstract. You drag it from To Do Work to Urgent Top Priority. After a third cup of coffee, you see the card sitting there in the Urgent column and just force you to get it done. Writing it under pressure was not pleasant, but at least you did not miss your deadline. After writing the abstract, you drag the card from the Urgent Top Priority column and drop it in the Done column. You sit there looking at the card, thinking "Glad that is done. Why did I agree to write that article anyway?" To reward yourself, you go outside to play kick the can. Or you go for a walk listening to Stive Morgan's "Mystical Wood" instrumental song. Or you take a nap. Trello helps you stay organized and can adapt to changes you need without having to retype anything.

Regardless of what you do after dropping the card into the Done column, in this example of the abstract, you managed the natural rhythm of your workflow and never missed a beat. Trello lets you create a workflow that can change with your changing circumstances, needs, and priorities. You can get all the things you need to get done onto a digital card. You clear your mind by moving all the clutter of to-do items onto a digital card that can be moved around your workflow board. A task goes from needing to be done, to being done, to sometimes becoming urgent, to being done. Sometimes the task languishes and loses importance or you just never feel like doing it. That task may end up trashed for another life. The flexibility of being able to move cards around to match your energy, time, mood, and shifting priorities, makes this workflow system a powerful method to get your thesis, journal article, or other writing project completed.

Evernote

Evernote is a program that helps you feel organized with your notes and makes them available wherever you are and ensures that they are synchronized across your devices. Evernote is a free program with lots of great free features but also has a paid premium upgrade option. We have used Evernote for years and consider it our go-to note taking and organizing app. It can help you easily capture and prioritize your ideas, to-do lists, and projects without losing anything anywhere. No matter which idea you captured, you can quickly search all your notes no matter where it is or how often it occurs across notes--even if the word being searched is written by hand in a picture you captured!

With Evernote, you can manage your thesis project and even small moments like inspired ideas for a vacation after you finish writing your thesis draft. You can capture your ideas in notes, voice, and pictures. The app is a single place for your notes, ideas, lists, and reminders. Access these using your desktop, laptop, smartphone, and tablet. All the devices synchronize and notes you created on your office computer will be available on your tablet or any other device. If you take a picture of a whiteboard schematic or even of a page in a book, it can be accessed and the words in the pictures can be searched on your tablet or laptop or any device that has your Evernote app installed.

The feature we use the most when we are working on one of our writing projects is the webclipper extension on my webbrowser. We use Chrome and Firefox, and both of these have webclipper extensions that allow us to save a clip or entire webpage to one of our Evernote notebooks (keep one notebook per writing project: they can be shared for collaboration—like we do). With the webclipper, we can capture a section of an article and save it to a project notebook. When working by myself, if I want the whole article on the webpage, I can select save article in the webclipper window that pops up after clicking the elephant icon that represents Evernote (you know the saying, an elephant never forgets). These clips are very convenient for capturing information and keeping them organized and accessible wherever I am on whatever device I am using. When you need to find the information quickly when talking to your supervisor or when writing, a search of your Evernotes will result in the clip showing up on your screen.

Install the application on your devices and install the webclipper on your internet browsers. Adding Evernote to your system of tools and techniques for writing your thesis and you will be done with it in six months or less.

Endnote

To produce your literature review without confusion, lost time, tears and anger, you need to use a bibliography management program. We suggest using Endnote. We have used it for many years. Suzanne used version 4 when writing her thesis. At the time of this writing,

Endnote 9 is available.

Back in the early 1990s I used a program called Papyrus. Back then I had to type out every entry into my bibliography management program. Today you can add entries with a couple of computer mouse clicks from Google Scholar, Web of Science, or from journal publishers' websites. Keeping track of your literature, producing reference lists that are correctly formatted for whatever style you need, and even maintaining digital copies of articles in your bibliography are so much simpler, better, and flexible today than when I did my dissertation. Endnote is necessary to writing your thesis in six months and making your literature review relatively painless.

Endnote has many features, but we will only touch on a few of them. Our goal is to get you started using Endnote so you can write a good literature review and painlessly produce your thesis. Teaching you how to be an expert user of Endnote or any other software tool we mention is outside the scope of this book. Your expertise in using Endnote, like other programs we mention, will come in time as you use the program and discover how its features make your life easier and better. If you want strong skills using Endnote, you can sign up for my Endnote course on Udemy. Email me at editor@americanproofreadingcenter.com for a discount coupon code. For now, let's cover the basics and get you started.

Endnote has a several features that make your thesis literature review and reference section easy and of high quality. First of all, you can import references from Google Scholar. Once the reference is in your Endnote library, you can search for available full text copies online with a single click within Endnote. If available online, the pdfs will automatically download and attach to your reference. Within Endnote, you can open a reference's pdf and read it, annotate it, and search it with keywords. When finished with your library, you can ensure its accuracy by refreshing it with a couple of clicks. The program will seek out any updates to your references. For example, if the publisher did not have an abstract available for your reference at the time you downloaded it but then made one available, Endnote will update your reference with the now-available abstract. Abstracts are an important part of creating an annotated bibliography you use to produce your literature review, so this updating feature is great and effortless.

You can use the Cite While You Write (CWYW) feature in Endnote to insert references from your library into your text document. I personally do not use this feature because I do not like to stop the flow of ideas when writing in order to mechanically insert a citation. If I know the citation off the top of my head I just write the citation and if I do not know the citation, I just type (add reference). Then I go back and do the mechanical editing of references as a batch activity. BUT, if you want to use CWYW, feel free to do so. Endnote makes it easy.

Besides making your literature review easier to produce by keeping your references organized, Endnote produces multiple reference sections as easy as clicking your mouse a few times. Because I used a bibliography program like Endnote when I wrote my dissertation in 1995, I had little trouble producing my reference section. Classmates and faculty told me not to forget how important it was to produce an accurately formatted reference section and that they did not envy me the task. I smiled and said, "Yes, it is going so hard. I will get it done though." They did not know that I had been typing out my references all along (back then I sat at my Gateway 386 desktop about an hour every night around 11pm typing out the references of the day). The effort paid off because when needed, I simply typed the commands and a completely accurate reference file was produced as a text file. I inserted the text file into my word processing program (Word Perfect--yeah) and I was done.

When you use Endnote today, the headache of creating your reference section goes away. In fact, when you need to create a reference section for one or more articles you will write based on your thesis, you will easily create it in exactly the format required. Few things delight a journal editor more than a perfectly formatted reference section and nothing gets your article submission sent back un-reviewed than a messed up reference section.

Endnote is worth the money you will spend getting it. Take some time to learn its features. The time and money you spend will be repaid many times through less frustration, less stress, higher quality reference sections and more robust literature review sections that result in fewer rejections. Add a reference once and use it over and over again in different publications and conference papers. There are competitors out there on the market, but I advocate Endnote based on my years of using the program. To make the most of your purchase, take my Udemy course on Mastering Endnote. You won't regret it.

Scrivener

Scrivener is used by authors who write screenplays, novels, technical manuals, and other manuscripts that are more than a few pages. Like Endnote described earlier, Scrivener will be useful to you not just in writing your thesis, but also in writing your journal articles. Therefore, when writing your thesis, you need to use Scrivener. You probably are using

Word, but stop. You need Scrivener. It does not cost much money (currently US$45) and using it will save you time and increase your writing quality. Scrivener is different and better than any other word processing program for writing an article, book, or thesis because all your document pages, notes, and research are kept in a single, easy to use computer-screen window. I am using Scrivener right now to write this book and you should use it to write your thesis and journal articles.

Your thesis will be organized as a single project in Scrivener. Your project is kept in a digital "binder" and will have document folders for each chapter. For example, you will have one collapsible folder for your Introduction chapter, Literature Review chapter, Methodology chapter, Results chapter, and Conclusion chapter. You may have other chapters depending on your specific discipline's tradition or the preference of your supervisor. Within each collapsible chapter, you will have several document pages (they look like tiny images of a page in the binder). Each "page" can be as long or short as you need. For example, in your Introduction chapter, you will have a page for each of the chapter sections called Problem Statement, Background, Theoretical Framework, Significance, etc. When you click on one of these page images in your binder, you will get a word processing window on the right to type or paste your text. You can (and should) have a separate page image for each heading in your chapter to help you stay organized and make the most of your kaizen notes. If, as you are writing, you think of another section you need, simply right click the chapter folder in the binder and click Add to create a new page for the new section. You also have a folder located at the bottom of your binder for research where you will keep all your research notes as well as web links for use as reference and follow-up. This prevents you from getting too distracted and disorganized while you write.

As you write, having all your research notes and resources available within the same program is extremely helpful and prevents losing track of thoughts as you write. If you need to look up some idea or detail but cannot remember where you wrote about it, you can use a keyword to find where in your Scrivener thesis project the idea occurs. This is hugely helpful when trying to make connections between items in your thesis. Also, you do not want to contradict yourself or talk about it differently than elsewhere in the thesis. If you have word count preferences for a single page/section of your thesis, you can set the word count target and in the lower right corner of the page's window you will see a colored bar graph showing your progress in reaching the target. In fact, if you select the whole thesis in the binder window, you will see how many words are in the thesis and a progress bar on how close or far away you are from reaching your target word count.

There is a list view that shows you the different pages nested under the thumbnail icon you choose (e.g. thesis, chapter). It lists all the pages under it and their status and progress (assuming you set a number of words for each document). This lets you see the growing progress in completing individual sections and the entire thesis. Seeing your progress is really encouraging and motivating. This leads to more desire to continue writing and to break through the difficult writing parts. Scrivener even has a distraction-free mode (remember your use of Pomodoro's to do focused writing?) that removes all the visual material in the window and maximizes the writing screen (pressing the escape or delete button brings you back to the normal user window).

These features lead to more productive writing, which means writing your thesis in six months is easier. If you decide one section of your chapter needs to be placed elsewhere in your thesis, moving that text is as easy as dragging and dropping the page image from one place to another in the binder. Scrivener enables you to stay focused while writing each day by making the process of writing easy to stay organized while you write. When your thesis draft is complete, you will do a simple export to Word using the Compile function to produce your final thesis draft in the Word format most commonly used by your university.

If you already started your thesis in Word, you can import your text into Scrivener. If you have chapters already created, simply put a hashtag (#) before the chapter title(s) and from within your Scrivener project, select File, Import and Split, and select the file you want to import. In the import window, be sure to place a hashtag in the box at the bottom of the screen that says "Sections are separated by:". The chapter headings with hashtags before them will be split into folders in your Scrivener project.

You can learn much more detail on how to use Scrivener to write your thesis and journal articles by signing up for my Udemy online course, "Write your Thesis in Six months with Scrivener ". To get a discount coupon code just for you, send me an email at: editor@americanproofreadingcenter.com. Because the coupon codes are unique, if your classmates or friends want a discount code too, have them send me an email and I will send them a coupon code.

Scapple

Scapple is a concept mapping program from the company, Literature and Latte. There are many concept and mind mapping programs available, but Scapple is designed with the writer in mind. Literature and Latte is the same company that makes Scrivener, and the two programs should be used together. If you have never done concept mapping, using Scapple is a great way to get familiar with the activity and get the most out of it. If you ever jotted down ideas on a piece of paper and then drawn lines between related thoughts, then you have experience with concept mapping, and you have the basic notion of what Scapple does. Instead of paper, you start digitally with Scapple and export your ideas to Scrivener for use in your thesis.

Using Scapple is an important element in writing your thesis in six months. The concept mapping you do with Scapple will help you create a great outline for your thesis with lots of detailed sections (remember the tiny page images I mentioned?) that guide what you will write from one day to the next and what you will think about while you create kaizen notes throughout the day. Ideas you capture and the connections you discover between ideas help you to produce critical evaluation in your literature review.

Concept mapping is a practice that takes advantage of your brain's natural, non-linear and schematic way of thinking. Usually when writing an essay for school, we are told we need to create an outline before we start writing. Then we are taught to think about our outline elements from the introduction, to the body, then the conclusion. We are told to create, essentially, a linear table of contents in list form that starts at the beginning of your essay topic and finishes at the conclusion.

Most people do not create outlines because thinking of a linear table of contents is so difficult and the linear approach we are taught in school is not natural to us. Our brains simply do not think this way. Our mind jumps from idea to idea like a bird flitting from one branch of a tree to another. Have you ever seen a bird or even a squirrel flit up a tree from the base to the top? Of course not. They go up the trunk then go side to side then up some more, maybe back down, and often jump to another tree entirely. That is your brain when trying to write an essay and that is how your brain will act when trying to outline your thesis.

Concept mapping with Scapple works with your brain, not against it. You start with a blank, digital canvas and start typing ideas. Who cares where they fit? You just let your mind flit around the thesis content you can think of just like a bird flitting around branches of a tree. Keep putting ideas down on the canvas until your mind comes to a stop and you cannot think of anything anymore. Remember Pomodoros? I suggest you concept map for 25 minutes, dumping your ideas onto the canvas. If you run out of ideas before your 25 minutes are up, keep at it. Push past the blankness in your mind and you will find you have more ideas lurking in your brain somewhere. After your Pomodoro time is up. Take a break for five minutes, get a cup of tea, coffee, Pepsi, whatever. Don't forget to stretch. Then do another Pomodoro.

In your second concept mapping Pomodoro, you are going to concentrate not on new ideas, but making connections among the ideas you put on your canvas. In Scapple, making connections is super easy. You simply drag one concept and drop it onto another and a connection line is created. You will probably need to move the concepts closer together, but don't worry about the attractiveness just yet. Beauty and map design clarity comes later. Study your ideas. How are some of them related? Which ideas go together and should be clustered together? Drag and drop those ideas onto one another. One of the ideas probably will be the parent node and others the child notes. What you end up with is a network structure of ideas. If the canvas is getting too cluttered, go ahead and rearrange your related ideas to make them next to each other relative to other clusters. You will be cleaning up your canvas for clarity. Networks can be beautiful and elegant, so do not be surprised if the concept map of your thesis or thesis section turns out to be something you feel like printing and hanging on your wall. In fact, printing your maps and putting them within eyesight of where you write is a great way to constantly remind yourself of the bigger picture, systems-view of your thesis.

When you are satisfied with your concept map, you can export it to Scrivener. By exporting it as an opml file (sounds hard, just click file, export, opml--simple), you can then import the map into Scrivener. The elements will show up in your binder for your thesis project (assuming you were in your thesis project Scrivener file). Now you have the basis of your outline and you didn't have to experience the mental pain of having to try and build your outline details in a numbered, linear list.

With your detailed outline generated by Scapple and Scrivener together, you can pick and choose which section you want to write each day. The problem of staring at a blank screen and suffering writer's block seemingly goes away. Also, you can look at your outline and choose a section to ponder throughout the day, producing kaizen notes for each of the ideas you come up with. You probably will ponder two or three sections and make kaizen notes for them, not just one section. Jump to the section of kaizen notes if you want to learn more about how these work and how they jump start your writing each day to produce paragraphs that turn into pages each and every day. These pages all start by having a detailed outline that you produce using Scapple. If you have not purchased it yet, do that now. You will wonder how you managed to get this far in education without it.

PART THREE

Getting Started

Having an essay, chapter, or entire thesis in need of editing requires that you first write something. But most of us think that we do not have enough time to write. We imagine that we need blocks of time dedicated to writing. When the demands of everyday life eat away at the blocks of time we reserved for writing, despair sets in. We feel that we will never get it done. But rest assured there is a solution.

The key to getting your writing done is to take advantage of time otherwise wasted. So whether on a small pad of paper or using your phone to take notes, make the time to write a few sentences that capture the idea you have before it disappears from memory. Turn wasted time into productive time. Several novelists used this strategy to write their first bestselling novel. I used the strategy 20 years ago to write my dissertation. You can too!

Getting words onto the blank screen or on a sheet of paper is a challenge for most writers, but writers.....write. If you want to complete your thesis or get an article published, then you must be a writer--and write. There really is no way around this fact. There are people that talk about writing, and then there are people that write. But how do you go from being the person who talks with friends and colleagues about writing a thesis or article at the coffee shop or office to being the person who writes? The answer is simple.

Just get some words written.

I know you might be thinking, "It's not that simple!" But becoming a writer is simple if you accept that a writer writes and that if you write, then you are a writer. The content you write may not be very good at first and you probably will throw much of what you write away, but why should you be any different from all successful writers? All writers throw away content. Crafting an argument is not linear and getting the right words to express your ideas is rarely accomplished on the first try. So just write. You will find that writing words, even nonsense, will open up your mind and more words will flow onto the screen or page. Some of those words will be worthwhile. I guarantee you that you will have more worthwhile content if you just write off the top of your head than if you spend your time talking about your writing or delay writing until you have the perfect outline or know exactly what you want to say and how to say it.

How does this work, you might ask? Strategy and working smart, not blindly. You need to know what your thesis outline is, cultivate it by regularly adjusting it as new ideas and insight occur to you. You need to build chapters using kaizen notes and master the ability to develop well-formed paragraphs using the SEE-I format. Essentially, you must approach your writing in an organized and deliberate fashion.

We explained the strategy and tools you will use in the previous chapters. In addition, however, you need to design a Writing Space and use a Writing Project Box. You need to actively manage your research project and the relationship with your supervisor. Let's find out more about these in the following sections.

Your Writing Space

The main thing a writer needs, according to Stephen King, is "a door that closes." There may be more to what you need for a writing space, but a functional writing space, used often, will allow you to write well with minimum distraction and maximum ease. For King, that space has a door that closes and prevents people from interrupting him.

You will find that as you get into the habit of writing, the need to write will start to nag at you. When this happens, you should figure out how to create a temporary space. For me, sometimes that temporary writing space is at the coffee shop with my laptop and noise cancelling headphones playing meditation sounds to drown out the coffee shop chatter, expresso machine hiss, and the whine of Frappuccino makers. With a laptop and headphones playing meditation music, I can get into The Zone. Other times I sit in my car during a lunch break and type on my laptop in the passenger seat. People walking by probably think I am crazy, but I don't care. When I need to get the ideas written up, I find a way to create a Writing Space no matter where I am.

But you need a routine Writing Space that is your primary place for writing your thesis. A primary Writing Space not only has an environment that is distraction free, but also plays a role in fostering your habit of writing. The act of going into your Writing Space acts as a cue triggering your routine to start writing. If you just write sitting on the couch in front of the television, that might work but it will not act as a cue and foster the habit of writing. Writing a thesis is a long journey and you need to develop helpful habits that promote your success, so create a Writing Space.

There are many kinds of Writing Spaces. What works for your supervisor may not work for you. What works for you might not work for your classmate. Everyone is different and that is okay. Take some time to think about what you like. Carefully design your Writing Space with habit formation in mind. What are the things in your Writing Space that will act as cues to trigger the routine of writing? What might be ways you can minimize distraction when you are in your Writing Space? How might you arrange your things commonly used when you write so that using them does not interrupt the flow of writing and otherwise pull you out of The Zone? For example, I put my eye glass case in exactly the same place to the left of my computer monitor so that switching between reading glasses and normal glasses is easy and I am never wandering around my home office wondering where I put my reading glasses. That is a terrible distraction and I might get irritated enough that I abandon writing for the time being. I put my coffee or tea cup to the right of my monitor and away from the mousepad so I know without thinking where my drink is. I use drinking jasmine dragon pearl green tea as a reward after my first Pom but I continue writing with a second Pom and drink the tea while I write. I don't want to look for my coffee cup. So it always goes in the same place to avoid being a distraction. Look around your space and think about the human factors like the two I just described and design your space with purpose.

You can explore Writing Space ideas by looking at pictures and tweets #Whereiwrite. As you build your habit, change your writing space to fit your growing needs and ways of writing. When you are away from your usual Writing Space, think of ways to quickly create one when you need to get something written. There will be times when you have thoughts on your mind, entire paragraphs and pages that just want to come out of your head, and kaizen notes are not going to capture them properly. Only a full writing session will do it. You will still need a Writing Space and with a bit of creativity and preplanning (Bluetooth noise cancelling headphones in your bag) you can create one that has minimal distraction and has a kind of "door that closes".

Your Writing Project Box

To write your thesis in six months, you need many things, and one of them is a project box. A Writing Project Box is literally a box. Adapt the box concept to your liking, but start out, at the very least, with a plastic box like a milk crate. In it you will put two or three books you are looking at while writing your thesis (not all of them!! Just what you are looking at for the next few days or single day). In the Project Box you will have an accordion-style file folder. In the file folder you will keep the small pieces of paper you use for Kaizen notes. The file folder flaps should be labeled with the basic chapter outline of your thesis. When you write a kaizen note, you can put it in the correct chapter flap and not worry you will lose it. When you print out articles, you keep them in your Project Box. You can put each article in the accordion file in the chapter section in which the article may be relevant. You can also just keep all the print outs together in Manila file folders or bound together with large binder clips. Believe me the bits and pieces of paper and print outs and other stuff that you produce can easily and quickly get mixed up and out of control. Your Project Box keeps things organized in one place. Mentally, the project box also gives you peace of mind that your thesis is not taking over your life because it is "contained and tamed" in the Project Box. You might not believe me, but if you think about some faculty you visited in their office and think about all the printed paper everywhere, you may realize they never learned to use a project box. When you are a faculty member, instead of your office looking like a paper bomb exploded in it, each major project you work on can be contained and tamed in its own Writing Project Box.

Your Project Box should also have a journaling notebook that is just for expressing your thoughts and feelings during your thesis-writing journey. Keeping the journal in your Project Box keeps those emotions contained and where they belong--which is not all over the place in your life's various facets. A journal of thoughts and feelings may sound too touchy-feely for you, and that is okay. But you still need it. You could do your journaling on a private blog if you want, but there is something comforting about writing by hand in a journal that physically closes. Any journal style notebook can work, but my favorite is that produced by Moleskine. Whichever journal you get, write in it when the mood strikes you. Put your frustrations in it. Complain about your supervisor in it. Complain about the lack of support your loved ones are giving you. Write about how your classmate or supervisor stole one of your ideas and is using it in an upcoming conference. Get all those negative emotions off your chest, out of your heart and stomach, and onto the page. You will feel better. No one but you ever need read what you write in your journal. The benefit of this journal of subjective thoughts is that you do not blow up (as much) at your loved ones. You do not use time you do not really have venting to your friends at the coffee shop or restaurant. You get bitterness onto the page and do not become passive aggressive or (please never) hostile toward your supervisor. Capturing these inevitable feelings in the journal allows you to psychologically move on to more productive thoughts, emotions, and writing. Keeping the journaling notebook in your Writing Project Box keeps it and the emotions it contains in their proper place, which is not dominating your life.

You might be tempted to make a Project Box digitally using Microsoft's OneNote or whatever. Don't. At least at first. Use a physical box. Make it durable plastic, not cardboard. A milk crate is perfect for most purposes. I had a colleague who wrote great sociology textbooks. They were so good he made more money from his textbooks than he did from his salary as a full professor of more than thirty years. He came to work each morning pulling behind him two milk crates on a collapsible carry-on luggage dolly. He used two boxes because--you know--he was revising more than one textbook at time! The man was an inspiration of how disciplined habit made difficult work successful and rewarding. He was almost always in a good mood and could laugh at most every stupid thing the university administration asked of him. Did I mention that he was also for many years my departmental head? Get a Writing Project Box and you will be on your way to successfully completing your thesis in six months. And publishing articles. And laughing with classmates and faculty about annoying irritants that come with the academic life. And succeeding! After you get familiar with the Writing Project Box-that-was-a-milk-crate, you can experiment and get a more expensive roller briefcase like the Swissgear Granada Rolling Case or something like it. But a milk crate is hard to beat as a Writing Project Box.

Get one and use it to stay organized and sane while writing your thesis.

You and Your Supervisor

The relationship you develop and maintain with your supervisor is a crucial part of writing your thesis and successfully completing your PhD or Master's degree requirements. Your supervisor's experience and knowledge will help you overcome the obstacles you will encounter during your thesis journey. He or she will help you stay focused and will, at least some of the time, support you and give you guidance.

Some supervisors are horrible, but often a poor supervisor relationship develops because a student does not understand the relationship and does not remain the manager of his or her own research project. I've seen students that expect their supervisor to answer all their questions, including basic questions that other university staff or students can answer—or Google. I've seen students submit poorly written thesis draft material that is full of spelling and formatting errors. I've seen students who think it is the supervisor's responsibility to teach them everything and even to provide them with a research project idea. Then they complain that their supervisor is horrible, evil, and just plain not helpful. What?

To have a productive relationship with your supervisor, you need to find a balance of what you are taking control of and what input your supervisor provides. This will change over time, so you also need to be flexible. Always be in charge of the management of your research project. Decide what kind of support and help you need for each phase of your time as a graduate student and each phase of producing your thesis. Once you are clear about what support and guidance you need, you can share these with your supervisor and talk about them to produce a set of mutually agreed upon roles and responsibilities. Continue to talk through these because things will change over time.

Flexibility and the ability to adapt are important to your relationship and success. All relationships change over time and require flexibility and adaptation to changing circumstances. Did your supervisor just have a child? She will not have as much time for you and will be more tired than before and will take longer than she already did to return draft chapters or draft sections. Deal with it. Did your supervisor just get placed on a fifth university committee? Is he trying to finish a book as part of his tenure and promotion dossier? Did she assume the role of department head? Associate Dean? Getting divorced? Buying a house?

Your supervisor goes through life crises and experiences work demands just like everyone else.

Your supervisor has limited time and energy to help you grow as a scholar. Your professor is often trying to juggle:

- Too many committees
- Too many students
- More classes than they want to teach
- Securing research grant money
- Publishing regularly to ensure retention and promotion
- A personal life.

When you are a thesis supervisor, you will struggle too! Therefore, be sensitive and aware of what demands your supervisor is under. Your flexibility and awareness will help you maintain a positive relationship that results in your completing your thesis and related PhD or Master's degree thesis requirements in a timely manner.

As the director of your thesis cruise ship, you need to create a plan. Talk with senior graduate students and recently hired junior faculty to get their advice on what to expect and things that worked for them. Google your questions and find answers online. Create a membership to the Doctoral Support Group in Facebook, which is a great resource no matter where in the world you are doing your studies (DSG is anchored by graduate students and faculty in Malaysia; they are a fantastic online community). From what you learn you will increasingly visualize your journey and plan ahead without having to ask your supervisor for all the answers (remember how busy they are!).

There are a few things you can do to be productive and well thought of by your supervisor. Drop in meetings are fine, but scheduling a meeting with a clear purpose and clear goals is better. Know why you are talking to your supervisor, what you need, what you are giving, and what the outcome of the meeting should be. Are you seeking a decision about something from her? Are you just sharing information as a status update? Create an agenda and send it to your supervisor. When you meet, make notes of what is being covered and what guidance your supervisor gives you. This is very important. You will forget the details of what she said and you will annoy her if you have to ask again. You can even email your supervisor the main points and finer details as needed. Be sure to include things she told you to do and what your next action steps are. Your relationship with your supervisor, like any relationship, will thrive or decay based on how well you communicate, negotiate, and collaborate with her. You want her to do what she said she will do, and you in turn must do what you say you will do. Be reliable, trustworthy to keep the arrangements you make, and be prepared for every meeting. If you are, you will find that instead of being a problem child to your supervisor, you will be her golden child that she tells her colleagues about.

You can improve your relationship with your supervisor and make your thesis experience more pleasant and rewarding by finding ways to make your supervisor a partner in success. Everyone likes to have some benefit from their work. A few ways you can get your supervisor to help you succeed are:

Choose a research topic that is in your supervisor's experience and interest.

- Seek a research or teaching assistantship under your supervisor to foster a stronger apprentice-like relationship
- Create a study group and support network so that you ask your supervisor questions only he or she can answer.
- Invite your supervisor to coffee or lunch to discuss your research and writing.
- If dropping in unannounced, bring tea or coffee for your supervisor. He probably will not tell you to go away.
- Give your supervisor drafts of your work that are free of spelling and grammatical mistakes.

Your Dissertation's Outline

We are providing you with a generic dissertation outline that you can start with, but your outline will be somewhat different based on your specific field of study. Details aside, approach writing your thesis with the end in mind and visualize your thesis using the following outline. In the next chapter we will explain each major section and how to approach writing them one by one.

INTRODUCTION

1. A General Description of the Area of Concern
2. Problem to be Studied/Purpose of the Proposed Research Project
3. Major Research Questions and/or Research Hypotheses
4. Definition of Important Terms
5. Significance of the Problem and Justification for Investigating It
6. Basic Assumptions
7. Basic Limitations

REVIEW OF LITERATURE

1. Historical Background
2. Theory or Discipline Relevant to Research Questions and Hypotheses
3. Current Literature Relevant to Research Questions and Hypotheses
4. Literature relating to specific variables
5. Literature relating to your combination of variables (your model of the variables, if any)

METHODOLOGY

1. Restatement of Purpose
2. Description of Participants and Human Subjects Consideration and Clearance (if relevant)
3. Description of Instrumentation/Measurement Procedures (not found in Humanities and Fine Arts)
4. Research Design
5. General description
6. Threats to internal/external validity
7. Operational definitions of all variables
8. Description of Procedures
9. Data Analysis

RESULTS AND DISCUSSION

1. Restatement of research questions (hypotheses)
2. H1 and results of data analysis answering question/hypothesis
3. H2 and results of data analysis answering question/hypothesis
4. H3 and results of data analysis answering question/hypothesis
5. Presentation of results
6. Descriptive statistics (if quantitative)
7. Primary statistical analyses (if appropriate)
8. Post hoc and other secondary analyses
9. Tabular data or graphs (if you have any, but visualizations even if you are doing qualitative research)
10. Discussion
11. Summary

SUMMARY AND CONCLUSIONS

1. Summary

2. Conclusions
3. Implications
4. Relate, Speculate, Integrate your findings
5. Recommendations for future research
6. Why your study was needed and contribution it made

REFERENCES/BIBLIOGRAPHY

You will use Scapple (described in Chapter 2 under Technology You Need) to brainstorm and concept map your thesis outline. Use the outline I wrote above as a starting point. The detailed sections in your thesis will be your details, not mine, and reflect how your study is unique. Your outline will grow and change over time as you write. What you want to say will become clearer as you write and by using Scapple and Scrivener to write your thesis, updating your thesis outline will be easy.

Now that you have a sense of the sections you need to write, let's look at how to build your chapters. In the next section we explain the necessity of writing as a form of thinking through your research project, the use of kaizen notes in more detail and how to break down long writing assignments.

PART FOUR

Building Chapters

There is only one fail-safe method, one not-very-secret and guaranteed trick that you need in order to build chapters and finish your dissertation: Write. We mentioned this in the Getting Started section and repeat it here. Prioritize the act of writing itself and write every day. Writing must become a non-negotiable part of your daily routine. A commitment to the writing process is far more important than genius.

Writing is thinking. Because writing is thinking, brilliant thoughts do not just appear on the page after long hours of arduous musing on a subject. In our experience, the best ideas almost always come about through the act of writing itself. Many people think that writing up research happens somehow at the end of the research process. They are wrong. The end result will be much better if you think writing is something that happens throughout your research. So write from the very beginning or start writing wherever you are right now in your research project.

Writing as you work through data collection and analysis will help you think through your ideas and help you figure out what is going on in the data, what things mean, and why. Often we do not know what we think until we write out our thoughts. If you treat writing as an important part of the research process, you will find that:

- Writing gets easier the more you do it and becomes a habit
- Small amounts of writing done every day really add up quickly
- Writing regularly allows you to capture the many ideas and insights that otherwise would be lost to memory
- Writing throughout the research process leaves you with a draft of material that simply requires editing and refinement for clarity and explanatory force.

Producing dissertation chapters takes time and is challenging. Everyone struggles with similar technical and emotional issues: procrastination, distraction, anxiety, structuring an argument, finding their voice, integrating theory and evidence. It's very hard work, this writing-your-dissertation thing. The trick is to not make it even harder by avoiding the work itself.

If you make writing a part of your work-week routine, there will be good and bad days. On the good days, the prose will flow out of you at a rate that you didn't think was possible. On the bad days, nothing that you write will seem good enough. The trick is to go with the ebb and flow of writing, to ride out the bad days.

You will often feel lost and frustrated and tired—uncomfortable. The successful writer knows that feeling lost, frustrated, and tired is just a part of the process of coming up with something great. If writing is thinking, then there are bound to be a few false starts and dead ends along the way. If you feel poorly about your ability to write, force yourself to write anyway. You will not only finish your dissertation, you will allow yourself the opportunity to work through complicated arguments and say something interesting or even something great.

Let's look now at how writing throughout your research process and the use of kaizen notes promote your ability to write every day and helps you improve your writing over time.

Short Writing Using Kaizen Notes

Writing, like speaking, is often a kind of improvisation. What we mean is when you write, what you want to say often becomes clearer to yourself. Then you write some more and what you mean gets even clearer. You begin to visualize concepts in your mind and the ideas you are writing start to connect with other ideas in your mind. Examples come to your mind that illustrate what you are trying to say. You find yourself describing these examples. Analogies may occur to you, and you write those down too.

But none of this happens if you only sit around talking about writing. Students and faculty I see at cafes talking about the chapter, book, or thesis they need to write often stress themselves out unnecessarily. Talking about writing, when you are not in the daily habit of writing, psychologically highlights the fact that you are not doing what you know you must do. This stress leads to further writer's block or to writing avoidance behaviors like studying the best software program to use (just use Scrivener--problem solved), the best notebook for capturing your ideas (Moleskine notebooks--problem solved), or the "right" location-so-you-can-concentrate-on-writing (there is no such thing, just places you make into Writing Spaces—problem solved).

But don't misunderstand me about talking about writing. Writers do talk about writing. But they talk about it as people actively engaged in the craft of writing. Writing groups are important components of writing well and being productive. But talking about writing is only a productive and rewarding activity when you are already in the habit of writing.

The use of kaizen notes is a means of getting into the habit of writing. This technique allows you to painlessly grow the number of words you write. With more words written down, you will have content that you can edit. Once you find yourself with enough content to edit, you will realize you now have "first drafts" that lead to second drafts and will result, eventually, in final copy ready for submission to your thesis advisor or a journal editor.

To write kaizen notes, get a small notebook with pages that easily tear off. But don't let finding the right notebook slow you down. I started my dissertation writing by taking recycled A10 pages from the computer lab, cutting them into quarters, and stapling them into little notebooks. Whatever. Just get some pieces of paper you can carry around with you.

Now get a pen or pencil. They are lying around everywhere. Worry about the "right" one for you later.

Wherever you find yourself, take out your notepad and pen/pencil....and write ONLY ONE IDEA in a sentence. Then go to the next page if you have a second concept and write it out as a sentence. You can write two or three sentences, if you really want to, but only if they elaborate on your ONE IDEA. Put your notebook in your pocket and go do whatever it is you were doing. Smile. Say hello to someone. Get a coffee or tea. Be happy because you are now a writer who writes. This may not seem like much at first, but think about it. If you get five ideas on five sheets of small notepaper, you have at least five paragraphs waiting for completion. These pieces of paper quickly add up when you keep writing your ideas down AS THEY OCCUR to you. You could be standing in the checkout waiting to pay for groceries, waiting for your child to get out of school, waiting outside your thesis advisor's office, sitting at home watching a show on TV, or in the lavatory. As long as you take the minute or two to pull out your notepad and pen and write the idea down, you will painlessly incorporate writing into your daily life. With a handful of these pieces of paper, you can now turn single ideas and sentences into paragraphs and pages of content.

Each day you will have some number of notepad papers with ideas captured (aka kaizen notes). Decide when you will elaborate on these ideas each day. When is not as important as the fact that you take time each day to expand on the ideas captured. This is an important second step to being a productive writer. You can expand using a notebook and pen or on a computer or tablet. If using a notebook, keep in mind at some point you need to get your words into digital format and no longer on paper alone.

Sitting with a computer or tablet with a keyboard, read through your ideas collected on the pieces of paper. Shuffle the papers and read them again. Sit and think about what you read. Try to repeat to yourself in your mind the ideas found on the papers. Shuffle the papers again and read them once more.

Looking at the first paper, start typing what you wrote and then use the SEE-I technique to help guide how you expand on the initial idea written. Your goal is to elaborate on the idea and turn a sentence into a paragraph. If you have more than one paragraph to write, great! Write on! If not, don't worry about it. Just go to the next piece of paper and elaborate on the idea written so you have a paragraph or more. Doing this a few times will give you a sense of your goal of converting single ideas on each piece of paper into one or more paragraphs on your computer. With that understanding taken care of, you need to master the SEE-I technique of writing paragraph after paragraph.

SEE-I stands for State, Elaborate, Exemplify--Illustrate.

State means you write your idea. Usually this is the idea you stated on your kaizen note.

Elaborate means you expand on what is meant or captured in the idea stated. Elaborating can run into several paragraphs because you are explaining what the idea means, what variation in meaning the idea can have, why it might be important, when the idea became important, or where the idea has often been used. Essentially, you are explaining what you MEAN after you stated the idea.

Exemplify involves describing examples of the idea. How has it been applied in other research you know about? Describe examples of the idea to show how it has been used elsewhere. These examples can show the diversity of the idea you mentioned in the elaborate step.

Illustrate requires you to create a visualization of some kind to help the reader "see" the idea in their mind. You can use an analogy or metaphor to illustrate the idea. You might literally show a graphic or diagram to show the idea in a generalized form. Often we do not have illustrations for all our ideas in academic writing, but keep in mind you want some illustrations whether analogy, diagram, graphic or other technique that helps the reader mentally visualize the idea.

After doing this, you must make sure you go back to step one and your little notepads and pen when you finish writing up your current pile of notepad papers. If you completed writing up an idea from a piece of paper using the SEE-I process, store the piece of paper somewhere. We usually keep them clipped with a metal binder clip and keep them in groups of one week at a time. Store all of the bound papers in an accordion-style file folder in your Writing Project Box (described earlier).

YOU ARE NOW A WRITER! So grab some pieces of paper or a small notebook with tearable pages, get a pen or pencil, and just get some words written every day.

Breaking Down Long Writing Tasks: Paragraphs to Pages

Writing many pages like that found in a thesis or book takes a strategy and clear organization. We already made clear the strategy needed and described techniques and tools you will use. For example, you will use Scapple to concept map your ideas, Scrivener to organize your sections into manageable writing portions, Pomodoros for focused writing, and the use of kaizen notes to get started with each focused writing session. You will pay attention to how your day falls into the important:urgent matrix and keep in mind the Pareto principle.

As we described above, the two pages a day minimum you will write are based on kaizen notes as your starter. You will use paragraphs as your basic building block to write your thesis page by page, section by section and chapter by chapter. Paragraphs will cascade from one to the next in a coherent flow that brings your reader on an intellectual journey with you as their guide. There are a few rules you need to keep in mind about paragraphs to make the journey a pleasant and rewarding one for your reader.

If there is ever a single, most important rule about a paragraph, that rule is you must keep one idea per paragraph. The paragraph usually starts with a topic sentence. Often this will be your kaizen note, but the idea in a kaizen note can span several paragraphs and even result in pages of text. Regardless, keep one idea per paragraph.

All paragraphs must have a topic sentence. They indicate in a general way what idea or assertion the paragraph is going to deal with. Although not all paragraphs have clear-cut topic sentences, and despite the fact that topic sentences can occur anywhere in the paragraph (as the first sentence, the last sentence, or somewhere in the middle), an easy way to make sure your reader understands the topic of the paragraph is to put your topic sentence near the beginning of the paragraph. Regardless of whether you include an explicit topic sentence or not, you should be able to easily summarize what the paragraph is about.

In essence, therefore, a paragraph is a collection of related sentences dealing with a single topic. Learning to write good paragraphs will help you stay on track throughout stages of your thesis (i.e. different drafts). Good paragraphing also greatly assists your readers in following a piece of writing. The entire paragraph should concern itself with a single focus presented in the topic sentence. If it begins with one focus or major point of discussion, it should not end with another or wander between different ideas. You can have fantastic ideas, but if those ideas aren't presented in an organized fashion, you will lose your reader.

Once you have your topic sentence written, you will develop it. You will elaborate upon it to make what you mean more explicit. You may even illustrate the paragraph's idea with a visualization. Try two or three of the following options to develop the idea in your paragraph. The list is also useful to help you expand upon the idea on your kaizen note.

- Use examples and illustrations
- Cite data (facts, statistics, evidence, details, and others)
- Describe what other people say by paraphrasing or using quotes
- Use an anecdote or story
- Define terms in the paragraph
- Compare and contrast your idea with other ideas
- Evaluate causes and reasons
- Examine effects and consequences
- Analyze the topic
- Describe the topic
- Offer a chronology of an event (time segments)
- Unity, Coherence and Adequate Development

To be as effective as possible, in addition to a topic sentence, a paragraph should contain each of the following: Unity, Coherence and Adequate Development. As you will see, all of these traits overlap. Using and adapting them to your individual purposes will help you construct effective paragraphs.

Coherence is the trait that makes the paragraph easily understandable to a reader. You can help create coherence in your paragraphs by creating logical bridges and verbal bridges. A logical bridge is when the same idea of a topic is carried over from sentence to sentence. Often subsequent sentences are written in parallel form. Your paragraph may have verbal bridges. These are key words that can be repeated in several sentences, synonymous words repeated in several sentences, pronouns that refer to nouns used in previous sentences, and transition words to link ideas from one sentence to the next.

The topic (which is introduced by the topic sentence) should be discussed fully and adequately. Again, this varies from paragraph to paragraph, depending on your purpose, but you should be wary of paragraphs that only have two or three sentences. It's a pretty good bet that the paragraph is not fully developed if it is that short. A paragraph that is one sentence long in a thesis is the kiss of death and will definitely make your supervisor or reviewer question your competence and readiness for an advanced degree.

When to Start a New Paragraph

You should start a new paragraph:

- When you begin a new idea or point. New ideas should always start in new paragraphs. If you have an extended idea that spans multiple paragraphs, each new point within that idea should have its own paragraph. Your Kaizen notes are a good reference to start with.

- To contrast information or ideas. Separate paragraphs can serve to contrast sides in a debate, different points in an argument, or any other difference.

- When your readers need a pause. Breaks between paragraphs function as a short "break" for your readers—adding these will help your writing be more readable. You should create a break if your paragraph becomes too long or the material is complex. When editing theses, I have seen a paragraph span two or three pages. This is too long! A half page is usually the longest you want a paragraph to run in a thesis. You can create pauses for your reader when you make some paragraphs short and others longer. The variation helps to create a kind of mental breathing for your reader, giving them pauses before they get tired.

- When you are ending your introduction or starting your conclusion. Your introductory and concluding material should always be in a new paragraph. Many introductions and conclusions have multiple paragraphs depending on their content, length, and the writer's purpose.

Transitions and Signposts

Two very important elements of paragraphing are signposts and transitions. Signposts are internal aids to assist readers; they usually consist of several sentences or a paragraph outlining what the section has covered and what will come next. Transitions are usually one or several sentences that "transition" from one idea to the next. Transitions can be used at the end of most paragraphs to help the paragraphs flow one into the next.

If you begin to transition into a new idea, it belongs in a new paragraph. There are some simple ways to tell if you are on the same topic or a new one. You can have one idea and several bits of supporting evidence within a single paragraph. You can also have several points in a single paragraph as long as they relate to the overall topic of the paragraph. If the single points start to get long, then perhaps elaborating on each of them is needed. Placing them in their own paragraphs may be better. Try not to worry too much about this in the beginning of writing out your kaizen notes because you will later edit your writing to make it more clear, concise, and coherent (following the rule of one idea per paragraph).

The paragraphs you create using kaizen notes and the suggestions we provided you will result, as we said before, in many pages of text. You now need to understand how these many pages of text form your thesis. The next chapter gives an overview of each thesis chapter and common considerations you need to pay attention to when writing them. Don't worry yet about polishing your chapters, just get them written. We will cover how to polish your first draft once you roughly build your thesis sections.

PART FIVE

Writing Thesis Sections

We provided you with a generic outline for your thesis in the previous section. The details will depend on the specifics of your discipline and your research project. For most PhD and Master's degree theses, you will have a(n):

1. Introduction
2. Literature Review
3. Methodology
4. Results and Discussion
5. Conclusion

A metaphor commonly used for the structure of a thesis is a sandwich. You open with the Introduction and close with the Conclusion. These are your two slices of bread. To hold all the content of your sandwich, these slices of bread should not be too thin. If they are thin, then they will be too weak to hold the contents of the sandwich and it will fall apart. They should not be too thick, either. If they are too thick with detail, the "sandwich" will stick in your reader's mouth and they will never get to the middle part. The content in-between the bread-slice chapters are your meat and vegetables (or fish or just vegetables—make the sandwich you want!).

The chapters in the middle provide fulfilling content and justify what you opened with in your introduction. For each chapter, you will similarly create a sandwich with an introduction (one half a page or a full page, typically) that shows what you are going to tell your reader about. You will close with a conclusion that wraps it up.

Do not make the conclusion of a chapter into a summary but conclude and synthesize the most important things stated previously. Your thesis conclusion should conclude the whole thesis. Often the thesis just verifies aims and shows the significance of the results, but your concluding chapter should also recap the key parts of the literature and the chapters.

When you are writing your thesis section, write the Introduction and Conclusion chapters last. Then you can write your abstract and finally the decide on your title once you are happy with everything else.

Let's look at each chapter in sequence. After reading this chapter, you will have a good idea of what should be in each thesis chapter, how they relate to each other like parts of a sandwich, and how to write them.

The Introduction

In your introduction, don't waste time. Get right to the point. You want to grab your reader's attention like an advertisement that intrigues a customer to look further at what is being offered. Therefore, say up-front what the problem is (your thesis statement), what other people have done, and how you have added to it. If the examiner understands the thesis after the Introduction, you are halfway to acceptance. Unfortunately, when editing theses, sometimes we have no idea what the point was until somewhere deep into the first chapter. Sometimes we still do not know until into the third chapter. Make your problem statement or thesis statement clear from the beginning.

Your introduction needs to show evidence of critical thinking. You are not just describing information. You are evaluating it and synthesizing it. Show this higher-level thought to your readers in the first few pages of your introduction. You want them to have a good first impression of you and make them confident in your ability to critically evaluate your work and the work of others. If you wait until page 75 before you show them this, you already lost them and you have a problem on your hands. You may not convince them you are PhD worthy even if what you say on page 75 is really good. They already made their first impression and that impression is difficult to change. You can make a good impression in the Introduction chapter not only by grabbing your reader with a clear problem statement, but by defining the strengths and weaknesses of your own research and showing how it can be improved. Be confident but modest in your description of the impact your research entails. Your research likely is not changing the world. Your research should be enhancing it in a particular way. State that enhancement with confidence and do not exaggerate.

Make sure the aim of your manuscript is regarding the thesis, and not of the initial research project. Many students begin their introduction with the tired phrase, "The aim of this research project is ..." which often indicates that the original project aim has not changed in the writing of the thesis. Your research project is finished. Therefore the overall aim is the aim of the thesis. Everything you write should take the perspective that the research is finished. When you include future tense words like "will" when you describe your research, this shows the reader you cut and pasted your research proposal text into your thesis. Many reviewers stop reading at that point. You do not want that. If you are worried about this slipping past you, we encourage you to send us an email to arrange professional editing at editor@americanproofreadingcenter.com.

The Abstract

Few abstracts are any good in the first draft. For some reason most PhD students struggle to write an abstract, and often it is written more as an introduction rather than a distilled version of the thesis. Remember that the abstract is the first thing that the reader reads, so if it is not focused on presenting the whole of the thesis, you missed an opportunity to get the reader on your side. If possible an abstract should be a page in length. It should outline the problem, the contribution, the most significant methods, briefly describe what was designed/modeled, what was evaluated, and what were the most significant results.

The following is a good framework for writing your abstract:

Purpose

–This thesis argues... (place your thesis/problem statement here).

Design/methodology/approach

– The research was framed... (include theoretical framework and key methods).

Findings

– Results show that....(insert key findings).

Research limitations/implications

– Research was limited to...(say something about the scope) and suggests that... (what is implicated by your research).

Practical implications

– The paper may help scholars better understand...(insert how the research findings can be used).

Social implications

Research findings help....(some statement about improving life or economy or whatever in some way that makes the reader think, "That's nice!").

Originality/value

– The research fills a gap in existing knowledge about...(your subject of study)...and suggests...(significance and value of your research approach/findings).

If you have not written your thesis yet, do not write your abstract. Well, you can if you cannot help yourself, just to feel like you have one. But you will likely throw it away. You need to write your abstract after you write your thesis in its entirety. Only then will your abstract be of high quality and include all the necessary information in a concise language.

The Problem

Your dissertation needs a problem statement or thesis statement. The two terms are often used to mean the same thing in a dissertation. They can mean different things though for smaller writing projects. Whichever term you choose to use, the statement itself will be specific, of correct scope (not too small for a dissertation, not too large), and shows up in the first pages of your Introduction. It will be a single sentence or a short paragraph. The statement cannot be answered by a yes or no question; it must be defended through argumentation. A clear thesis or problem statement helps the reader know right away what your research is all about. It also helps keep your writing relevant. As you are writing, you might drift off into material irrelevant to your thesis. The problem/thesis statement helps you to check whether what you are writing belongs in your thesis or not. Your supervisor and reviewers will certainly be using it that way.

You should be able to make a connection between what you are writing each day and your thesis statement (outlining through concept mapping helps this too). If you cannot find the connection to your thesis statement, you can edit your writing (file it away for use elsewhere) or adjust your thesis statement if it truly needs to be revised. In addition to using it as a guide while you write, you will use it again when you are compiling your full first draft and editing out everything that does not contribute directly to your thesis/problem statement.

The Writing Center of Harvard University suggests that a thesis is never a question, list, vague, confrontational, or combative. Nor is a thesis statement an opinion or a statement of fact. A thesis, they say, should be a definable, arguable claim and should be as clear and specific as possible. After editing hundreds of theses for graduate students just like you, we agree.

The best way to get a sense of what a good thesis statement is for you is to look at completed dissertations available in your library. Look for dissertations that are in your discipline and look at how they did, or did not, state their argument succinctly. Just because a thesis gets accepted and deposited does not mean it is a good reference or even a good thesis. It just means they managed to get it accepted and deposited. So use your critical thinking abilities and dissect the thesis/problem statements you find. Look at dissertations from other disciplines, not just your own field of study. You need to get a sense of the variation. How does a thesis statement in literature look compared to one in computer science? How does one look in physics compared to sociology? Agricultural science and fine arts? Write down examples you like and examples you hate. Make a list of the good, the bad, and the ugly. These are great references and will help ensure you craft a great thesis statement for your research project and the opening paragraphs in your dissertation.

The Theoretical Framework

Many students get confused about theory and theoretical frameworks, but you can overcome your confusion if you keep things simple. A theory is basically a model of ideas that are formulated to explain, predict, and understand something. A theoretical framework is a set of concepts that are related to each other in some way and are used to organize the way you describe and explain your research. A framework does not cover everything that the theory describes, explains, and predicts, but just your research study. Think of the framework like a picture frame. What you see inside the frame is what is covered in your study and what is outside the picture frame (literally everything else) is not covered in your study and is said to be outside the scope of your study (this relates to limitations).

You know what a framework is because you see them all the time. If you see a coat tree standing next to a door, you have the basics right in front of you. A coat tree is a framework because it has different arms or branches held together by a single pole that is secured to the floor. Together, the different branches hold a variety of coats or jackets. You can think of each branch as an idea or concept in your theoretical framework. Swapping coats for data, you hang your data along the branches, which are all tied together and relate to each other in some way (namely your theory). Your data has organization and is related to each other in important ways and is not just a mass of data. A mass of data would look like a pile of coats on the floor. You know the pile of dirty laundry on the floor in your room? That's your data without a theoretical framework. Your theoretical framework provides the structure needed to understand the data, which without a framework will look like a chaotic mass.

There are a number of advantages to a good theoretical framework.

- Theoretical frameworks bring clarity to your research. Your supervisor and thesis reviewers can use it to critically evaluate your research.
- The framework provides a useful scaffold for connecting your research to other research and what is already known. The gaps in knowledge become very clear when you can show them through a theoretical framework. It also gives you a logical basis for your choice of research methods and your hypotheses.
- The theoretical framework you create allows you to go beyond describing phenomena to generalizing and explaining them.

The limits of your research, what is in it and what is outside of it, become very clear and easily pointed out. Too often we read theses that talk about limitations in a few sentences and focus on how their research is limited, deficient, or something seemingly negative. Yes, forms of sampling bias are limitations. But limitations are more importantly what your research is limited to in the sense of boundaries: what is in the framework and what is not in the framework. This is crucial because many reviewers will criticize your research but will stop criticizing in your viva voce when you point out that what they are stating is outside the limits of your research and they need to comment on what you researched through your theoretical framework. Criticisms about things not in your framework become the basis of recommendations for future research, which is an extension of how far your theory can be used to describe and explain phenomena. Instead of being confrontational with your reviewer, you can say something they argue about is outside your framework but is a great opportunity for future research.

With the description and explanation we gave you above, it should be clear to you that you need to create a theoretical framework. Here are some strategies to help you develop one:

- Examine your research problem. The research problem anchors your entire study and forms the basis from which you construct your theoretical framework.
- Brainstorm key variables in your research. Which factors contribute to the presumed effect? In other words, what are predictor (independent) variables and what are outcome (dependent) variables?
- List the constructs and variables that might be relevant to your study. Group these variables into independent and dependent categories.
- Review related literature to find answers to your research question.
- Review the key theories that were introduced to you in your coursework and choose the theory or theories that can best explain the relationships between the key variables in your study. Discuss the assumptions or propositions of this theory and point out their relevance to your research.

Like you did for learning to write a good abstract, go to your graduate library and look at dissertations from your field of study and map some of the theoretical frameworks you find. Do not be surprised if you cannot find a theoretical framework clearly articulated. Not all dissertations are of equal quality just like not all faculty are equally brilliant or helpful. When you browse dissertations, just keep in mind that a theoretical framework is used to limit the scope of the relevant data by focusing on specific variables and defining the specific viewpoint (framework) that the researcher will take in analyzing and interpreting the data to be gathered, understanding concepts and variables according to the given definitions, and building knowledge by validating or challenging theoretical assumptions. By clearly describing, explaining, and justifying your theoretical framework, you will probably be in the top 20% of all theses deposited. The effort is well worth the trouble. Go for it!

Significance

The significance section in your Introduction and Conclusion chapter describes the contribution your research project makes to the literature you reviewed (filling a gap) and several other considerations. These can include, for example, timeliness, economic benefit. Maybe your research provides needed insight regarding early detection of viral diseases in oil palm trees and the result will noticeably reduce the death of oil palm trees and limit the spread of the disease in a plantation. Maybe your study provides a cost efficient way to test the quality of refined oil. Maybe your research helps mariculturalists to reduce the cloudiness (turbidity) of fish ponds using readily available agricultural waste fibers. In these cases significance is a practical contribution and promotes translating theory-based research into practice and application. Maybe your study provides a unique synthesis of variables to understand how a diverse population gives meaning to changing concepts of gender. Your significance here is about putting together variables not previously merged to explain something that social and behavioral scientists have studied for a long time. At the end of the day, your significance section will tell the reader how you make an original contribution to knowledge, extend what is currently known, and how that originality and extension are valuable or beneficial to your target audience.

Literature Review Language

Do you wonder what your literature review should sound like? You will be surprised to know that even experienced scholars can dread writing the literature review section of their article or book. Most students start off thinking a literature review is a listing of ideas various scholars published about a topic. Many students jump right in to their literature review by cutting and pasting sentences they come across while reading articles and books, fooling themselves in the process by saying they will paraphrase it later. When I was working on my first literature review thirty years ago, I often stared at published paragraphs (no internet yet!) feeling desperate because I couldn't think of how to say it better or how to paraphrase it. Suzanne struggled with this as well. Everyone does at first. The trick to literature review language is to think in terms of a conversation, not a list of ideas.

Imagine you are at the coffee shop with other people interested in your topic. You are all talking about your subject and arguing about it. You say Author 1 claims one thing, and your friend says "Yes, but

Author 2 claims the real issue is another thing". You ask "Why would Author 2 say that?" and the third person in your coffee shop group says "Because Author 2 shows that X and Y are examples of how the real issue is this other thing." Not convinced, you point out that Author 3 claims Author 2 used faulty results to show X and Y are the examples of the real issue and that Authors 4 and 5 further corroborates Author 1's findings through a study from another part of the world. This coffee shop argument results in a structure like: you said, he said, she said, you said, they said. A literature review is just an organized argument from different authors about ideas. The following questions can be used as a starting guide for structuring your organized argument of they said/I said (i.e. your literature review)

- Who are the most senior, established scholars of the subject?
- Who are new and emerging voices writing about the subject?
- What have scholars said about a subject?
- Which are the points most accepted by most scholars?
- What are the points upon which some or many scholars disagree?
- What is the strength of evidence for points upon which they disagree?
- What are the elements about a subject that few scholars have explored?
- When did scholars examine the subject and how has the way in which the subject was studied changed over time, if at all?
- Where has the subject been studied and how have those different places been used to show important insight about the subject?
- Why is the subject worth further inquiry now?

And, most importantly, what do YOU have to say about each of the elements above....what are YOUR thoughts on the subject? You need to have a voice in the literature review just like you would have your own voice in a conversation/argument at a coffee shop. Don't be afraid to say what you think. Your contribution is how each of us contributes to the growth of knowledge and information.

For more detailed and thorough guidance on how to painlessly write your literature review, look for our forthcoming book entitled, Painless Literature Reviews and take our Udemy course. For less than the price of dinner for two at a modest restaurant, you will get hands-on learning that makes your literature review painless and a pleasure to read. For more information, email us at editor@americanproofreadingcenter.com.

Methodology

We do not know which discipline you are coming from or what specific methods you used in your research, but we can help you be thorough and clear in writing up your methodology chapter (or section, depending on what your supervisor wants). Thorough means everything important is found in the chapter. Clear means you describe your methods clearly with the right words. Your goal is to be so clear and thorough that another researcher can reproduce your study, build upon it with another study, or accurately evaluate whether you used the best methods for the results you wanted based on previous explanations of your theoretical framework.

The first step is to make sure you are thorough in what you write about. To make sure you do not forget to write about something important, start with brainstorming in Scapple. Brainstorm all the methodological steps and issues on the Scapple canvas. Then organize the ideas on your Scapple canvas into groups or clusters of ideas. These clusters form your section headings. Related concepts are sub headings. With your concept map completed, import it to your dissertation project in Scrivener (again, see the section on Scapple for how to do this, but we encourage you to take our Udemy short course on using Scrivener and Scapple together to write your thesis and journal articles. Send us an email at: editor@americanproofreadingcenter.com for a discount coupon code).

While writing the content for each of the sections, you must be sure to write clearly. Methodology can get crazy. Sometimes we write out what we did and it is confusing to a reader. Try to avoid words with four syllables or more. Keep it simple and try to say what you did in plain language without using jargon as a short cut to describing or explaining what you did.

Creating flowcharts, illustrations, and other forms of visualization is important in a methodology section or chapter. Many times when we are editing someone's thesis, they describe what they did using too many words: pages and pages of words. Often a flowchart would be so much more meaningful to the reader and less effort for them to understand. If you cannot draw a flow chart of what you did, you probably do not have a clear enough understanding in your head of what you did. Using Scapple to make a flowchart and brainstorm it will solve this problem. A visualization in your own mind is really important to speaking about it clearly in your viva voce or just casually with your supervisor. Take the time to make visualizations and use them in your methodology section.

You can then use fewer words to describe what you did, which makes reading and understanding your methods easier for reviewers and your supervisor. The less effort and struggle they experience reading your thesis, the better off you are and the closer to acceptance you will be.

Your methodology needs to be justified, not just described. Take the time and get through the discomfort and difficulty of explaining why you chose one tradition of data collection and not a different tradition. Your justification should not be overly brief and should show the reader that you really understand, for example, why qualitative data were most appropriate and why quantitative data through survey instruments were not going to help you answer your research questions. Why, for example, is a phenomenological approach best and empiricism not insightful? Why did you use one type of experimental design and not another? You probably have something to say about novelty of methods used to study your subject. Be confident and explain it. If you can clearly cover the philosophy of science behind your choices and approach, you will be in a great position. Your methods are tied to your theoretical framework, research objectives, and research questions discussed in your first chapter. Make the connections for your reader. Again, the easier you can make it for your reader to understand what you did and why and how your research project elements are all connected, the better off you will be. If you can do this, trust us when we say you will be in the top 25% of thesis writers. If you can do it clearly and thoroughly, you will be in the top 10%. Using Scapple, Poms, and kaizen notes coupled with daily writing sessions will get you there.

Writing your methodology

Regardless of which discipline you are in, you will need to describe and explain how you did your research and why you did it that way. This relates to epistemology, which is basically the study of how you know what you know. So how do you know what you know in your research? Answering that question is your methodology and it needs to be well organized for clarity and conciseness.

You should discuss not only the methods you used, but also the methods you did not use. Start with the methods you chose to use in your research and justify why they were logical choices. You will want to cite the methods used in other studies that were similar in some way to yours. Once you complete writing about the methods you used, write about the methods you did not use. Explain why they were not appropriate. You need to cite the methods used in other studies and how they resulted in rather different things than what you are interested in. Using this approach helps to ensure that your discussion of methods does not sound like something copied from a methods textbook.

The methods section can be organized in many ways, and different disciplines have different styles. If your research is based on one experiment, for example, your methods might be contained in a single chapter. If your research is based on several experiments, you likely will report your methods in several chapters: one chapter for each experiment. If your study is coming from the arts or humanities, you may discuss methods primarily in your introductory chapter.

To get a good idea of the standards and conventions for your discipline, gather ideas for your methodology chapter (and other chapters in your thesis) by looking at other theses completed in your discipline. Where are the methods talked about and at what level of detail? How did the author (someone who was just like you at the time of writing their thesis!) justify their methodological choices? How did they explain why they did not use other kinds of methods?

Analysis section

Describing your analysis is often part of describing your methodology and focuses on how you processed your data rather than how you collected it or the philosophical-scientific traditions you are working within. Sometimes describing the analysis goes along with your results section. Where they go depends on which academic discipline you are in, the research tradition you are using, and your supervisor's preference. Regardless which chapter your discussion of analysis is placed, you want to be clear and thorough like you were for your methodology section. Using Scapple to do mind mapping is also the best way to achieve thoroughness. The use of visualizations is the best way to help ensure clarity.

Once you write out which analytic techniques you used, refer back to the bibliography you created for your literature review. Do not leave a "literature review" only to that section. You want to contrast and compare your ways of analyzing your data with the ways data were analyzed in the published literature. Did you use the same or a similar technique as someone else? Why? What did you hope to achieve by using the same technique? Did you modify a technique based on someone else's technique? Why? What did you hope to achieve by modifying the technique reported in a publication and why was modification rather than duplication the better approach? Place your analysis in a wider body of techniques; your reader wants to know you are familiar with a variety of analytic techniques and wants to ensure you are aware of how you choose the right technique for the right result with reference to your theoretical framework and research objectives.

Your analysis may be new and significant. Be sure to speak about how your analytic techniques are novel and significant. This can certainly be the case in the harder sciences and computer science. Do not just say what you did to compute your results. When appropriate, confidently show how you extended an analytic approach or developed a new technique using emerging technologies or the creative synthesis of existing technologies and methods.

The Results and Discussion Chapter

Reporting the results of your data analysis is much more than just saying what resulted. You need to explain what the results mean, which means you need to find and tell the story in your data. You will report your findings, for sure. This will be tables of data results, perhaps, showing things like R squared values and significance. Your results may show frequency of terms used by informants to demonstrate the common concepts or ideas they talked about. These are quantitative results of qualitative data to support your assertion that there were, for example, five primary themes in key informant narratives. Maybe you have tabular data showing tensile strength of concrete pylons used to anchor buildings or brittleness ratings of asphalt mixed with oil palm fruit fiber waste. All these data need to be clearly presented and a story woven using your research objectives, research questions, hypotheses, and theoretical framework as your guide posts for what to report and what not to report.

Your first step is to find the story in your data. To do this, you must really, really KNOW your data. You are the master of your data. No one should ever know your data better than you. It is your dissertation data, after all. During and after you conduct your analysis, take notes on what the data mean. Remember your kaizen notes and writing throughout the research process described in the beginning of this book. Look at the data and think about it. Does it answer your research questions? Which hypotheses are supported by the results and which hypotheses are not supported? Why would this be the case? Are there confounding (unknown and unmeasured) variables that are influencing your results or accounting for some amount of variation when you conduct an analysis of variance? If you are doing qualitative research in the social or behavioral sciences, what is not being talked about in your transcript data? Was the absence of certain concepts surprising to you? Why? Interpret your data early and often, approaching it in cycles or iterations. This much time with your data and thinking about what they mean will make you expertly familiar with the results and help you start to see a story in the data.

Another way to find the story in the data is to once again use concept mapping. Doing this in Scapple will help you see the bigger picture of your data and will help you see how individual results may be related to other results. Use concept mapping to depict the bigger picture. You might even use your concept map in your thesis because your supervisor and reviewers will benefit from the bigger picture and the ability to see "the forest for the trees". The concept map of the results has additional benefits. The map helps you to stay grounded (connected) to your data when you are interpreting it.

You need to use your theoretical frame to help you remain within the scope of your research project. You do not want to make interpretations that have nothing to do with your theory. Refer back to your problem or thesis statement often. Look at your theoretical frame, research objectives, and research questions. These are guide posts for making sense of your results.

Use Pomodoros to answer for yourself what you have learned from the data. What do you know now after analyzing the data that you did not know before you analyzed your data? Use kaizen notes to answer that question. Use Pom-based free-writing sessions to fill out and elaborate on your kaizen notes. In the kaizen notes, you can even use 3x3 or 3x5 sticky notes because you will write only one sentence per kaizen note. Then you can organize the sticky notes into groups by sticking them on a large wall or dry erase board. This is similar to what you do when using Scapple to do concept mapping. This use of sticky notes is something we use frequently in Design Thinking workshops and is called Affinity Diagramming. Once you have the sticky notes grouped on the wall or dry erase board, write a heading label for each grouping of sticky notes. These groups and their headings help you to plan how you will write up what you know (discovered from analyzing the data) in the discussion section of your results chapter. Do this regularly and often so you do not forget important insights. By writing throughout the research process, you will clarify for yourself what you now know.

When you are on your mental journey to discover your data's story, you should start with your theoretical framework, hypotheses (if you have them), and research questions. These provide you with the elements of storytelling. When using your hypotheses, state them, test them with your analyses and then discuss what is implied by the results of the tests. You can also approach your story's structure in an analytic way. You can start with the key concepts you used in your study (just like you might have started with your hypotheses--it depends on the kind of study you are doing and the discipline you are in). How do the findings make these key concepts more understandable and the substantial issues you studied? In doing either of these approaches, you maintain the sense of a story by maintaining sight on the bigger picture (the Affinity Diagraming/Concept Mapping described above) and making connections between the key data elements and key concepts and showing the patterns that emerge from your analysis and answering your research questions. You then will be making connections to broader theory and research described in your literature review.

When discussing your findings, you need to develop the story you found in the data. How much discussion is necessary depends on which discipline you are in, but all disciplines to one extent or another require interpretation that is based on making sense of the connections among the results. Most likely, you will discuss the major findings that came out of your research and how these relate to what you originally proposed. You can ask yourself, do your findings support or not support your hypotheses and why? Is one or more hypotheses only partially supported and why would this be and in which ways? Were any hypotheses disproved or unsupported? Why would this have happened? Did you discover anything that you did not originally expect to find out? How?

You wrote a literature review chapter, but you also need to relate your findings fit into other work done in your field of study. Where do your data agree or disagree with research done elsewhere? What alternative explanations of your data are possible, not just the interpretation you are promoting. Where are these alternatives found in the literature? You can explore your bibliography in Endnote. Use it to go back and forth between other people's research and your own (think of a she said, they said, I said style). Using kaizen notes and free-writing, answer the following: what has been done by other people, what has been done by you, and how do the two complement or conflict with each other? Keeping these three clear and distinct from each other will make reading your discussion of results easy for your supervisor and reviewers and therefore more successful.

Despite the wide variation in the way different disciplines tend to approach how to report and discuss research findings, you will at the very least need to be able to maintain focus on the research objectives, questions, and any hypotheses. You must also stay within the limits of your theoretical framework. When writing up your results, you are doing more than reporting the data that emerges from collection and analysis. You are also making connections between and among data. You will be saying why one or another patterned way of understanding the data is best. This is your interpretation and using techniques described above will make the process clear and achievable. You will complete it in a reasonable amount of time without tears or gray hair resulting from the experience.

Writing Your Thesis' conclusion

Your conclusion is not meant to be a summary of what you wrote throughout the thesis. Your conclusion is also not a miscellaneous chapter where you can say whatever you want and go off on a tangent that is not clearly related to your research, problem statement, or theoretical framework. There is some summarizing, yes. But you will be making a mistake if you just copy and paste content from the introduction and other chapters to build your conclusion. Your thesis' conclusion is just that: a conclusion...as in you concluded, came to a conclusion, figured something out, this is what it all means. That is a conclusion. If it was a summary, we would call the chapter Summary, not Conclusion. Keep in mind, however, that some reviewers will never read your entire thesis and will go straight to your conclusion to get an idea of what your research project was all about. They may read only until they think of three or four questions to ask you during your viva voce or oral defense.

You must draw out key aspects of the literature you studied along with your recommendations and say how they are justified or contradicted by your research. Your conclusion will remind the reader of what you researched (problem statement), how you researched it (theoretical framework and methods used), why you researched it (filling gaps in existing research and knowledge and issues of timeliness and originality), what you discovered or demonstrated (your results), and why anyone should care (the significance). Think of this portion of your thesis' conclusion as the initial speech you will give at your viva voce. So do not cut and paste. Rewrite it and be able to speak it confidently.

Your conclusion will discuss limitations and the significance of your research. Refer back to what I said about your theoretical framework. Having a good framework makes clear your limitations and reduces your tendency to dwell on failures in your research and what it cannot explain or predict. Discuss what was included in your research and what was left out and how these things left out are good items to consider in future research you or someone else may conduct.

By selling your research through clear presentation of what was done, how, and emphasizing the contributions it makes to knowledge and the discipline, you set yourself up well for describing how your research is significant and result in several recommendations that emerge from your research. You should brainstorm with smart people in your social network a set of recommendations on how your research findings can be applied, used and extended. Thinking of recommendations is sometimes easy and obvious. Sometimes it is difficult. Do a collaborative brainstorm to generate lots of ideas to get a few great ideas for recommendations that emerge from your research. Just be sure that the recommendations are supported by the scope and outcomes of your research. Take your justifiable recommendations from the brainstorm and write them into your conclusion.

Whatever you do, do not approach your conclusion as an afterthought. It should not be a short chapter. A short conclusion is a sign of laziness and a lack of caring about your research. A short, poorly written conclusion can lead a reviewer to choose between minor corrections and major corrections. Take writing your conclusion seriously, use the guidelines mentioned above, and you may find yourself going from minor corrections to exemplary.

PART SIX

Polish Your 1st Draft

Congratulations! You made it this far! You used kaizen notes and focused writing sessions using Poms to write pages each day and over three hundred pages in six months. You used strategy to maximize your 80/20 rule potential and worked most of the time in the important but not urgent quadrant. You tracked your tasks using Trello and leveraged other software to help you work to your fullest potential. You have a thick stack of printed text for each of the chapters in your thesis and now you need to edit it for submission to your supervisor.

When editing your thesis, keep in mind that above all else regarding your writing, the purpose of scientific writing is to convey information, nothing else. Your thesis can and should be a joy to read, but that joy should come from clearly and concisely conveying information, not creatively entertaining the reader. There is room for creativity and even storytelling in some disciplines, but not at the expense of communicating research.

There are several considerations to keep in mind in preparing your thesis' first draft. These include:

1. Keep your message clear.
2. Create a logical framework. This is why you used Scapple to

produce a concept map of your thesis and its subcomponents.

3. Be confident in your material: you have a good problem statement, theoretical framework, methodology, and interesting results. State what is new and important upfront. Do not bury these points at the end of your text.

4. Avoid dull language and cut, wherever possible, words that end in "tion" and use active verbs instead.

5. Explain your research simply. There's nothing nicer for an examiner when the candidate takes a complex idea and gives their own viewpoint on it, in a simple way, using new material. It shows that the student can articulate complex ideas in a simple way. The standard test for any thesis is that a 14-year old child should, at least, be able to read it and understand some of the key concepts in it.

Every piece of writing has a specific audience. In your thesis, you are writing for your supervisor first and foremost and your committee secondarily. You are not writing for your classmates or your discipline writ large.

Get Professional Editing Help

You will need the assistance of a professional academic or scientific editing services company. You wouldn't believe the number of PhD thesis' I have read that have a typo in the very first line of the thesis or even the title! A supervisor or examiner becomes annoyed if they have to keep correcting typos, and the more annoyed the reader, the more time they are taking away from actually reading the content.

Getting professional help will cost money and it will not be cheap, but you will recover your money in the time and expenses associated with taking longer to complete your submission requirements. If a poorly edited draft given to your supervisor or examiners delays you by three months, how much did those three months cost in rent, food, and other expenses? We are sure the cost is less than what professional editing will cost. So using professional editing makes good economic sense and gives you peace of mind when you submit your thesis draft.

You need to contact a company that offers copy-editing, formatting and in-depth scientific editing of manuscripts using native-English editors. Do not use the cheapest editor you can find. Not all editors are equal. Quality is often more expensive, but that is true of most everything from food, to cars, to watches, and to universities. Pay the money required to use a well-regarded editor who is a native English speaker and writer. This is important because there are many ways that language can be technically correct but "sound" wrong and awkward. These wrong-sounding words and phrases irritate the reader and cause you to resubmit after re-editing your thesis.

You want to look for companies that provide a basic service, including correcting for grammar, spelling, punctuation, consistency, clarity, proper capitalization, accurate use of terms and logical presentation. Many services also correct for British or American usage and for adherence to particular style manuals, such as the Chicago Manual of Style, the American Medical Association or the American Psychological Association. AmericanProofreadingCenter.com, for example, provides all of these services and in addition specializes in editing theses and articles by authors whose first language is not English.

Brevity is Vigor!

Prepare your first draft by editing your pages for clarity and impact. E.B. White wrote, "Brevity is Vigor!" in his classic, *The Elements of Style*. His statement is hard to follow for most writers of academic articles and theses. Graduate students usually think first about how many pages they need to write before they think they are finished with their dissertation.

Think about structure: Subject, Verb, Object

My most embarrassing moment in graduate school involved the lack of clear writing. Not long after I returned from collecting ethnographic data in the Philippines, my research supervisor read part of a chapter. I went to see him in his office. I was optimistic. I can still see myself standing in front of his desk asking him if he had time to read what I wrote. He looked severely at me over his large nose and bushy black mustache, bald head shining in the sunlight. "Marcus" he said. "What language is this written in?" Flushing in embarrassment, I said, "Um." He held out the sheaf of papers toward me across his desk. "Your writing is not clear and sometimes I wonder if it is in English or one of the other languages you speak." "Um." I stammered. "The cat sat on the mat" he said, raising his voice. "Subject, verb, object: can you write like that?" "Um." I said, wondering if this was really happening to me. "Good!" he said, thrusting the dozen or so pages of my partial chapter at me. "Write like that and then bring it back to me when finished!"

He was harsh, to be sure. Embarrassing me was not necessary. But he did make his point and made it well. I've never forgotten to think about the basic structure of a sentence. At its simplest, a sentence has a subject, a verb, and an object. There are elaborations using conjunctions and clauses and all kinds of forms only a grammarian could keep track of or care about. Sentence structure is broken with artistic license. But the basic building block is subject, verb, object. Fill your paragraphs and pages with this form and you will be, if nothing else, clear and concise. In Chapter 3 we explained how to break down long writing tasks and how to use the SEE-I technique for building paragraphs and a logical flow between paragraphs that each contain one main idea. Refer back to that section when you need to remind yourself how to do it.

When looking at your draft thesis papers and to help avoid the embarrassment, ask yourself, "Would I say this in normal speech?" Never mind the fact that the way we speak every day is full of pauses and incomplete sentences. Focus on the tendency to use simple words rather than complex words. Simple is clear. Clear is understandable. Understandable is more likely to be accepted by your supervisor or journal editor rather than rejected.

Reduce wordiness

You can make your writing more concise by eliminating phrases of the form it + be-verb or there + be-verb. The most common kind of unnecessary sentence construction involves an expletive (it was, there are) followed by a noun and a relative clause beginning with that, which, or who. In most cases, concise sentences can be created by eliminating the expletive opening, making the noun the subject of the sentence, and eliminating the relative pronoun.

Use verbs when possible rather than noun forms known as nominalizations. Sentences with many nominalizations usually have forms of "be" as the main verbs. Using the action verbs disguised in nominalizations as the main verbs—instead of forms of "be"—can help to create engaging rather than dull prose.

Other Considerations for Clarity
- *Do not write long sentences.* A sentence should not have more than 10 or 12 words and preferably never more than twenty words. A sentence with more words than that should be divided into two sentences. You can usually look for the word "and" for the location to make the split.

- *Each sentence should make a clear statement.* It should add to the statement that went before. A good paragraph is a series of clear, linked statements. Remember the SEE-I format we described to you.
- *Do not use big words.* If your computer tells you that your average word is more than five letters long, there is something wrong. The use of small words compels you to think about what you are writing. Even difficult ideas can be broken down into small words.
- *Never use words whose meanings you are not sure of.* If you break this rule you should look for other work. We are being harsh when we say this, but think about it. If you use words in your thesis that you do not know the meaning of, you literally do not know what you are talking about. An examiner will crush you. Be safe and use words you understand.
- *The beginner should avoid using adjectives, except those of colour, size and number.* Use as few adverbs as possible.
- *Avoid the abstract.* Always go for the concrete.

Practice Academic Honesty: Avoiding Plagiarism

Honesty is the keystone to academic work. The strength of your presentation and contribution are worthless if you plagiarize or misuse data.

The best way to avoid problems that result from plagiarizing is to always write ideas in your own words. Instead of copying and pasting, think about what the passage means and then write it down and cite the source when you are finished. Not only will you avoid punishment from the University, you will understand what was said and why you are using it. With this writing strategy, you can easily explain your work to your supervisor and defend it successfully. For added peace of mind, contact us about scanning your draft for plagiarism.

If you used the strategy and techniques we provide you in this book, you will have only a normal amount of plagiarism to worry about. This is the amount of text that slipped through without reference while you were writing using kaizen notes and so on. Plagiarism only becomes a big problem when whole chunks of your thesis are literally copied and pasted from other texts and not written in your own words. The strategy we provided you in this book prevents this from happening, so use our strategy and techniques. As part of your quality control and effort to polish your first draft, scan your thesis against the Turnitin database. Your university probably has a license to Turnitin, and you can scan your thesis for free. If not or if you do not want to use their system yet, you can always contact us at editor@americanproofreadingcenter.com and we will scan your thesis for you. We can also edit and proofread your final thesis draft.

Formatting Your Thesis

Before you print and submit your thesis, you need to get it edited and formatted. Be sure to get it professionally edited. We talked about what you need to look for in an editor in the previous chapter. We edit theses and journal articles every day of every week. Visit our website to learn more about our editing services that help you get published and get your thesis accepted. Our address is: https://www.americanproofreadingcenter.com. It is full of useful information that you want to look through.

Formatting is difficult and is also something you should pay someone else to do. Your university has specific guidelines regarding formatting. These guidelines are meticulous and can be quite irritating to follow if you do not understand how Microsoft Word's desktop publishing tools work. Don't waste lots of time and endure frustration to save a bit of money.

Your local print shop at the university or near it is a master at your university's formatting requirements. They can do in minutes or hours what will take you days if not a week or more. Their formatting will also be perfectly correct, whereas your formatting will still have errors that irritate your supervisor and reviewers. Pay the print shop to format your thesis. They may even format it for free if you print your copies with them. They may have a package price. Pay your money to get your thesis professionally formatted and printed. While your thesis is being professionally formatted, use your time for more productive and rewarding tasks that you are good at. Or just go have a nice afternoon with your friends or loved ones. You deserve it after having written and polished a thesis! Celebrate!

Epilogue

Y ou finished it! Having a polished full draft of your thesis in your hands is a great feeling. Enjoy it!

After sending us your thesis for professional editing, you can now get it printed at your local print shop. After handing the printed copies to your supervisor and sending it to your reviewers, we hope you will go for a great lunch or dinner. You might be wondering though, "What now?"

The answer is: Kaizen. Continue to improve.

Doing what?

Improve your bibliography. Remember the law of the harvest: what you reap is what you sow. Continue to regularly look at research in your area of study. Add relevant references to your Endnote library of research references. Cultivate your garden, so to speak, by removing items that are not useful, add more notes in references to improve your bibliography in Endnote. Doing this will keep you fresh and current and well-prepared for any revisions your supervisor or committee asks you to make.

Publish an article or two based on your dissertation. Refer to your Scapple concept maps to find elements you can pull together and use to structure journal articles. You can take our Udemy course on how to write a journal article based on your dissertation thesis. For a discount coupon code, send us an email at editor@americanproofreadingcenter.com and we will send a code just for you.

Publish a review article based on your literature review chapter and annotated bibliography.

Finally, **celebrate that you completed your thesis draft within six months.** You achieved something great and created a piece of scholarship no one else would have created like you did. Enjoy the first full step you took on the road to being a lifelong learner and scholar. Stay in touch with us and let us know about your journey. We'd love to hear from you!

Dr. Marcus B. Griffin
Dr. Suzanne Griffin
editor@americanproofreadingcenter.com

A Personal Request

If you enjoyed *Write Your Thesis in 6 Months* and found it useful, may we ask you an important favor? Please take a minute to go to the book's page on Amazon and recommend it to other readers.

Book sales at Amazon and the ability to find a book at Amazon is based on a search algorithm. The algorithm is brutal. If a book does not receive a large number of good reviews, then Amazon buries the book and it becomes almost impossible to find even if you use the right keywords.

The algorithm does not read what you post on Amazon; it only counts the number of reviews a book gets and the star ratings it accumulates. That is why an Amazon review does not have to be long and can be just two sentences or a few words about how our book helped you.

What matters to Amazon is that you take time to review a book and that you give *Write Your Thesis in 6 Months* a star rating that tells other readers you enjoyed the book. Doing this will help other readers find our book and learn how they can write their thesis in six months.

We would be grateful if you take two minutes right now and post a short review on Amazon if you think other readers will benefit from our book.

Thank you, very much!
Marcus and Suzanne

Meet Dr. Marcus B. Griffin and Dr. Suzanne Griffin

Marcus and Suzanne Griffin are former professors who discovered that they enjoy helping students and faculty around the world in multiple universities more than from working out of one university campus.

Drs. Griffin & Griffin have lived and worked in America, The Middle East, and Asia for over thirty years. They regularly travel and work from Jordan, Kuwait, the United Arab Emirates, Korea, Japan, Thailand, Malaysia, the Philippines, and the United States.

Marcus and Suzanne run the AmericanProofreadingCenter.com and regularly email customers and readers a few insights about teaching and learning in different parts of the world and provide tips and other suggestions for how to learn effectively and succeed in the Academic Life.

Please consider adding your name to the list of readers and customers who are already receiving Marcus and Suzanne's newsletter.

Go to https://www.americanproofreadingcenter.com

www.ingramcontent.com/pod-product-compliance
Lightning Source LLC
Chambersburg PA
CBHW021231280526
45784CB00005B/2053